• A HISTORY LOVER'S •
GUIDE TO
DETROIT

KARIN RISKO | *Photography by Rodney L. Arroyo*

THE
History
PRESS

Published by The History Press
Charleston, SC
www.historypress.net

First published 2018

Front cover: Rod Arroyo.
Back cover, left to right: Rod Arroyo, Bedrock, Library of Congress.
Maps courtesy of Chad Bianco.

Manufactured in the United States

ISBN 9781467135672

Library of Congress Control Number: 2018948037

To Jean,
yours in history!
Karin Risko

Dedicated with love to Baylee and Stefan.
And in loving memory of Tracy Savage and Charles Risko.
Hard to believe you've been gone five and ten years, respectively.

CONTENTS

Slow Roll, a weekly cycling event drawing thousands of cyclists, takes over Cadillac Square. GM RenCen can be seen in the distance, First National Building in the right foreground. *Courtesy of Bedrock.*

ACKNOWLEDGEMENTS

A sincere thank you to:
Krista Slavicek (former History Press acquisitions editor), Ben Gibson, Hilary Parrish and the entire History Press team for making this book not only look good but turning it into a reality.

Rodney L. Arroyo, owner of Portraits by Rod and City Books and Photos, Inc.

Family, friends, acquaintances, colleagues, businesses and subject matter experts who offered insightful tips, photographs, clarification, design assistance, proofreading/editing help, moral support, etc.: Blake Almstead, Dan Austin, Bedrock, Chad Bianco, Charley Bohland, Elizabeth Bohland, Bruce Butgereit, Carhartt, Danielle Center, Ken Coleman, Bill Dickens, Karen Dybis, Bobbie Fowlkes-Davis, Natalie Gray, Gail D. Hershenzon, Jamon Jordan, Michael Keropian, Kathryn Luna, Rachel Lutz, Luke McGrail, Marion Miele-Christiansen, Patricia Mischel, Dave J. Moore, Gail Offen, Michele Picchi-Babcock, Candi Randazzo-Boik, Bridget Risko, Robin Schwartz, Sue Schleicher-Shoemaker, Nancy Senatore, Kimberly Simmons, Steven Stanford, Kelly Walter and Charlie Worden. My apologies to anyone I missed.

A special shout-out to my Detroit Tigers experts: Kathy Azzopardi-Bridges, Michael Bsharah, Suzette Daye, Bob Hatline, Jonie Holland, Carrie Hutchinson, Andrew Johnson, Tim Kaminski, Chuck Mickiewicz, Susan Mierzejewski-Flores, Paula Portelli, John Rutherford and Kim Stafford. Without your input, "the corner" at Michigan and Trumbull would have been just another corner!

INTRODUCTION

Detroit is popping up on all kinds of popular travel lists as *the* place to visit. After decades of negative press, the recognition is appreciated. The influx of visitors, curious to see what the buzz is all about, is a welcome boon for local attractions and businesses, including mine. Requests for private and public tours have soared in the past two years.

There is something rather comical and even disconcerting, however, about these lists. They tend to portray Detroit as some "new discovery" and imply that there was nothing in Detroit worth seeing or discovering until the city emerged from bankruptcy, a pricey watchmaker (no offense, Shinola, we love you) and other oft-touted new businesses opened up shop and investors became interested in the city. This narrative couldn't be further from the truth.

While many think the trendy art, food and cocktail scene, new sports stadiums and redevelopment projects are the big draws, they're just part of the story—the icing on the cake. Yes, hip coffee shops, restaurants, bars, distilleries, microbreweries, boutiques, urban gardens, galleries and funky street murals do elevate the travel experience. They're what draw visitors and make for an exciting stay. These leisure and lifestyle amenities can, however, be easily replicated anywhere. What makes Detroit truly an exciting destination—unlike anywhere else—is its unique soul, story, history.

The flags of three different countries—France, England and the United States of America—have flown over Detroit, one of the Midwest's oldest cities. Antoine de la Mothe Cadillac claimed this region for New France

City on the rise waterfront view features a bustling wharf with steamships from Tashmoo Park and Bob-Lo Island, favorite local amusement parks, and signage for homegrown staple Vernors Ginger Ale. *Courtesy of Library of Congress.*

seventeen years before the French lay claim to historic New Orleans. Our nation's Founding Fathers declared independence from Britain seventy-five years after the creation of Fort Pontchartrain du Detroit.

Sainte Anne de Detroit, established two days after the city's French founding, is the second-oldest continuously operating Catholic parish in the United States. Detroit served as a major stop on the Underground Railroad. Its residents played a pivotal role in securing Union victory during the Civil War, while local politicians authored major legislation that still defines our nation.

Not only is Detroit known for putting the world on wheels, but it's also known as the "Arsenal of Democracy." During his December 29, 1940 fireside chat that was broadcast live over the radio, President Franklin Delano Roosevelt warned listeners of the dangers Americans would encounter if Britain fell and the Axis powers prevailed. "We must be the great arsenal of democracy," he implored after urging manufacturing facilities to begin producing defense materials without delay. The Motor

City answered the call by suspending automobile production at its factories to make jeeps, tanks, bombers and other military equipment instead. By producing 30 percent of the nation's munitions, Detroit shaped the outcome of World War II.

Civil rights leaders and labor activists organized massive marches and protests here. Their activism brought about significant social changes in the country. Sports legends such as Joe Louis, who was raised in Detroit, and labor leaders such as Walter Reuther not only left marks in their respective fields but also impacted American history.

Detroit's storied sports teams, dating back to the early days of their prospective professional leagues, have long drawn visitors, as have the city's distinguished cultural institutions. The Detroit Institute of Arts ranks among the finest art museums in the nation, and the Detroit Symphony Orchestra is a world-class orchestra. Prior to the recent opening of the National Museum of African American History and Culture in Washington, D.C., Detroit's Charles H. Wright Museum held the distinction of being the largest repository of African American artifacts in the world.

It's no big secret Detroit is synonymous with music. Home of the world's oldest jazz club, it's here where many legendary jazz and blues artists met fame. The Motown sound, the soundtrack to so many lives, still endures. Rock greats, the Queen of Soul and the first family of gospel all hail from Detroit, where the music legacy continues today in the contemporary forms of the genres mentioned, as well as hip-hop and techno.

Tourism is nothing new to Detroit. The *Illustrated Guide and Souvenir of Detroit* published in 1878 by Silas Farmer & Co. lured visitors with this enticing description: "This Queen City of the Lakes, the oldest in the West, is rich in legendary lore and rare historic story."

The nation's first convention and visitors bureau opened right here in 1895, and the "spectacular Detroit International Exposition & Fair of 1889 put the growing, pre-automotive city in the glare of the international spotlight, drawing attention to the metropolis' potential, progress, and prosperity," according to author Richard Bak. The local tourism industry became so competitive by 1915 that tour operators fought over who would take sightseers to popular destinations of the time, such as the log cabin at Palmer Park, Belle Isle and Waterworks Park. Smaller companies accused Dietsche Sightseeing Company of using unfair practices to gain advantage, such as anchoring "a sightseeing car to Woodward avenue and using it as a decoy to get passengers."

Tour bus belonging to Dietsche Sight Seeing Company, one of many tour operators providing tours of Detroit in the early 1900s, stops in front of Belle Isle casino. *Author's collection.*

Even world-famous Gray Line bus tours could be found in Detroit. The company, which started in Washington, D.C., in 1910, expanded into major cities including Detroit in 1926. A few years later, the city's transportation department became a Gray Line franchisee and continued operating the service. Aside from a brief closure during World War II, visitors could see the city aboard Gray Line buses until service was discontinued without fanfare or much public notice in 2003. A 1965 advertisement billed the tours as the "most complete and appealing ever assembled." Destinations on the two- to five-hour tours included Greenfield Village and Henry Ford Museum, the waterfront, Civic Center, Belle Isle, Windsor, New Center area, Wayne State University campus and cultural center.

For most of my lifetime, this great city has been viewed with derision and fear. The dramatic loss of population, industry and jobs during the latter half of the twentieth century resulted in an unfathomable decline of a once great American city. This prolonged downfall caused many serious issues, including financial instability, which eventually led to municipal bankruptcy and an unprecedented amount of urban decay as thousands of buildings around the city sat vacant.

Sadly, over the years, it seemed as if many people took pleasure in Detroit's demise and used it to validate political ideology and racial views.

The media didn't help matters by pushing images of Detroit's decline and decay in practically every article or feature. In the early twenty-first century, people came to Detroit specifically to gawk at the ruins and learn nothing else about the city. Like many others, I became weary of this jaded depiction and began giving tours to combat these one-sided portrayals. Now as the tide shifts toward positive coverage, people are clamoring to discover Detroit and are surprised to find out the city is much more than what they previously read or heard. I'm fortunate to be in the position where I meet people from all over the country and world and tell them Detroit's great story—the good, bad, pretty, ugly, strife, scandals, successes, etc. I've discovered that even after telling it a thousand times, Detroit's story never gets old.

I hope as you navigate your way around town, you find this guide easy to use. It should help you make sense of the historic buildings, beloved landmarks and noteworthy attractions you'll encounter. While *A History Lover's Guide to Detroit* is a labor of love, trying to fit this fantastic city's history into thirty-five thousand words or fewer was stressful and impossible. I purposely didn't delve deeply into Detroit's decline and racial divide. If you'd like to learn more, many other books do a great job of tackling these complicated subjects. If I left out significant people, places, industries or events, I apologize. Book a tour with me, and I'll tell you the whole story.

Most importantly, I urge you to take the time to thoroughly explore the city's past and enjoy all the fun new developments unfolding today. While people love to talk about reimagining or reinventing Detroit, I hope you take the time to rediscover it.

CHAPTER 1

LOOKING BACK

Detroit is known worldwide as the Motor City and has long held the distinction of being the "automobile capital of the world." While the automobile wasn't invented here, Detroit was the place to be to make your mark in the industry. During the first half of the twentieth century, over one hundred automobile manufacturers and suppliers were located here. Henry Ford's launch of the Model T, implementation of the moving assembly line to produce affordable cars and five-dollar-a-day wage revolutionized the industry. Today, the metropolitan Detroit area is home to what's known as the Big Three: Ford, GM and Chrysler (technically FCA for Fiat Chrysler Automobiles).

Detroit's thriving auto industry fueled the creation of many other supporting industries, and the plethora of job opportunities brought people here from all over the world. Its rise propelled the importance and need for labor unions such as the United Auto Workers to protect workers' rights and provide living wages. It gave us the first mile of concrete highway and the first traffic light.

As important as the auto industry is to Detroit's legacy, that's only part of our story.

July 24, 1701, is commonly claimed as the birthdate of our city, but that's really just the beginning of our European history. Although they left little evidence of their lives, it's believed Paleo Indians, a nomadic people who were primarily hunters-gatherers, inhabited this region thousands of years before French colonization. Seventeenth-century French explorers and eighteenth-century settlers would have encountered Native American tribes such as the Odawa or Ottawa, Potawatomi, Ojibwa, Huron or Wyandotte, Menominee, Fox, Miami and Sauk.

Native Americans found this area desirable because the rivers, streams and dense forests provided fertile hunting and fishing grounds. The interconnected waterways made it easy for early inhabitants to travel throughout the area. Many of our major roads, such as Jefferson, Woodward and Michigan Avenues, follow the routes of early Native American footpaths.

The abundant wildlife—primarily beaver, as their pelts were in demand—drew French explorers and trappers to claim this area for France. When Antoine de la Mothe Cadillac and his entourage arrived in the area on July 24, 1701, they established Fort Pontchartrain du Detroit, a settlement that served as both a fort and trading post. A lucrative fur trade was established between French fur traders and local Native American tribes. It's from this early fort that our city derives its name. *Detroit* is the French word for "the strait."

To attract families to the settlement, the French government offered free land to colonists. By the early 1760s, the population had grown to nearly one thousand, making Detroit the largest European settlement between Montreal and New Orleans. Life was difficult in those early days, but many hardy French settlers saw opportunity and chose to join the fur traders. They established ribbon farms, which were long, narrow strips of land originating at the river and stretching miles inland. Many Detroit streets follow the boundaries of those early farms and are named for the original property owners.

French settlers brought cuttings of their beloved pear trees to the new settlement, and these trees flourished. Early written accounts from visitors frequently mention these trees, which lined both sides of the Detroit River. As recently as the 1930s, a dozen trees, dubbed the Twelve Apostles, stood near the river in an area that later became Waterworks Park.

Great Britain, victor of the French and Indian War that pitted British colonists against those in New France, gained control of Detroit in 1763. Under British rule, Detroit served mainly as a fort. Although Great Britain ceded the territory that included Detroit to the newly established United States as part of the Treaty of Paris of 1783 that officially ended the Revolutionary War, the British didn't relinquish control until after the Jay Treaty was signed in 1795.

After the 1794 defeat of the British-supported Native American Alliance during the Battle of Fallen Timbers by American troops led by General Anthony Wayne, Native American tribes relinquished claims to

An artist's rendering of Detroit in 1819 depicts Fort Shelby and neighboring homes located within a stockade. *Courtesy of Library of Congress.*

Fort Detroit and the surrounding area the following year with the signing of the Treaty of Greenville.

Even under American control, Detroit was not a popular place to settle due to its remote location. The swamps and forests made this mosquito-laden place especially unattractive. The completion of the Erie Canal in 1825, however, opened the West and made Detroit easily accessible. Cheap land made this once unattractive area desirable. With the discovery of natural resources such as iron ore and copper in Michigan's upper peninsula, Detroit's location between the raw resources and major markets made it convenient for investors to set up shop. The advent of the railroad system created an even greater boon for Detroit.

By the mid-nineteenth century, Detroit had transitioned from a sleepy military outpost to a bustling port city and industrial hub. Industry thrived, and wealthy Detroiters made their fortunes from a variety of ventures, including lumber, agriculture, cigar production, steel and railroad car manufacturing, pharmaceuticals and shipbuilding. In the latter part of the century, Detroit became known as the stove capital of the world.

While many believe the automobile made Detroit, the industrial boom in the late nineteenth century created a sizeable wealthy class, many of whom were eager to invest in the fledgling and risky concept of motorized vehicles. In addition to accessible funding, the infrastructure needed to manufacture ships, railroad cars, stoves and steel was already in place and could easily adapt to automobile production.

Detroit's economic upturns resulted in building explosions that harnessed the talents of world-class nineteenth- and twentieth-century architects. The contributions of Daniel Burnham, C. Howard Crane, Paul Cret, Cass Gilbert, Albert Kahn, Louis Kamper, Gordon Lloyd, George Mason, Eero Saarinen, Mies van der Rohe, Wirt C. Rowland, Stanford White and Minoru Yamasaki can be found throughout the city. Famed landscape architect Frederick Law Olmsted and skilled artisans Marshall Fredericks, Carl Milles, Corrado Parducci, Mary Chase Perry Stratton and Ezra Winter are credited with beautifying the city.

Manufacturing propelled Detroit's growth, creating not only a wealthy elite but a sizeable middle class as well. The rich built elaborate mansions, many of which stand today, and provided funds to build beautiful churches reminiscent of their European counterparts. They amassed great works of art, and their collections can still be enjoyed today. Many used their fortunes for commercial ventures, creating grand skyscrapers such as the Fisher and Guardian Buildings or beautiful movie palaces such as the Fox Theatre. This

A night view of the prestigious Detroit Athletic Club with Ford Field, home of the Detroit Lions, in the background. Gem Theatre and Music Hall are to the right. *Rod Arroyo.*

wealth found its way into city coffers, paving the way for the creation of beautiful municipal parks and innovative city services.

The heavy emphasis on manufacturing, particularly automobiles, during the twentieth century has been detrimental too.

"Like no other city in the USA, Detroit reflects the triumph and tragedy of America's automotive age, which dawned at the turn of the last century," writes Stefan Link, assistant professor of economic history at Dartmouth College in "Detroit: Capital of the Automotive Age," a December 2015 blog post at globalurbanhistory.com.

He describes early 1900s Detroit as a modest and typical midwestern town, firmly embedded in the vibrant agro-industrial economy of the Great Lakes Basin.

> *Then came Henry Ford and the automobile: together, they launched Detroit onto a hundred-year trajectory of first astonishing rise and then equally stupendous decline.*
>
> *At its peak, Detroit was a city whose industry and architecture radiated worldwide. And like a distorting mirror, Detroit reflects in strange but recognizable form the experiences of many other "car cities" in the age of the automobile: migration, labor strife, postwar affluence, and post-Fordist crisis.*

Professor Link and many other economic experts attribute Detroit's current plight to the industrial restructuring of the global economy, a process that began in the 1970s and has accelerated since. Why didn't other twentieth-century car cities experience the same urban decline as Detroit? Wolfsburg, Germany, home of Volkswagen, for example, was identified as Germany's richest city in 2013. According to Professor Link, the contrast demonstrates that "social dynamics and political decisions," as well as economics, factor into whether a city survives or declines.

"Detroit's 20th century boom created an industrial monoculture in Southeastern Michigan that left workers few alternatives once crisis hit. Detroit's poverty is also owed to 'white flight'—the typical migration pattern that has eviscerated inner cities in the US since the 1970s: move beyond 8 Mile, Detroit's northern border, and the white suburbs begin and average affluence rises."

Although a global population explosion and the rise of East Asia's economic power have completely transformed the auto industry, "the automobile industry remains one of the most important sectors of the world economy—in employment, value-added, and in its spill-over effects into construction, oil, and engineering. It is worthwhile to recall the unlikely locale where it all started: around 1900, in Southeastern Michigan, in an unremarkable Midwestern town called Detroit."

The fallout from industrial restructuring, rapid suburbanization and discriminatory social and political dynamics of the last century was catastrophic. Once ranked the nation's fifth most populous city in the 1950s with 1.8 million residents, the population had dropped by 60 percent as of the 2010 census. The shift of jobs and population eroded Detroit's tax base. As a result, the city filed for Chapter 9 bankruptcy on July 18, 2013, the largest municipal bankruptcy filing in U.S. history by debt. The city emerged from bankruptcy in December 2014.

Today, Detroit is a work in progress. The downtown area is a sea of construction as historic buildings are renovated and new projects are underway. Some progressive developers are expanding construction projects far from the gentrifying areas in hopes of serving as a catalyst to revive those neighborhoods. So when you visit, don't expect Detroiters to be in a constant state of despair or mourning for what once was.

As Detroiters work to reestablish their place in the world, they optimistically look forward to new innovations that will rebuild their beloved city just as has been done many times in the past—this time with much more diversity and inclusiveness in hopes of avoiding the pitfalls of the past. They take inspiration from the city motto penned by Father Gabriel Richard after the city was destroyed by fire in 1805: *Speramus Meliora. Resurgent Cineribus*. "We hope for better things. It will rise from the ashes."

A FEW DETROIT FIRSTS

1. Vernors Ginger Ale, invented in 1866, is believed to be America's first soft drink.
2. The first convention and visitors bureau in the country opened here in 1895.
3. Our nation's first aquarium opened on Belle Isle in 1904.
4. The first mile of concrete highway was laid in 1909 on Woodward Avenue between Six and Seven Mile Roads.
5. Automobile Laundry, the first automated car wash, opened in 1914 on Woodward between Palmer and Hendrie Avenues. Workers manually pushed cars to the different stations. Wash and polish cost $1.50.
6. The country's first tricolored electric traffic light was installed in 1918 at the corner of Woodward and Michigan Avenues.
7. The Detroit Symphony Orchestra was the first in the world to broadcast live over the radio in 1922.
8. Detroit Police Department was the first to dispatch radio broadcasts to police cruisers in 1928 after the first police radio dispatch system was developed in Detroit.
9. The Detroit-Windsor Tunnel opened in 1930 and is the first automobile tunnel designed for traffic between two countries.
10. The nation's first sports bar is reputed to be the now-defunct Lindell A.C., which opened in 1949.
11. Paint-by-numbers, a revolutionary art craze that swept the nation in the 1950s and '60s, was created by Detroit native Dan Robbins for Craft Master, a division of Palmer Show Card Paint Company.
12. The rotary die encapsulation machine invented by Robert Pauli Scherer in the basement of his Kirby Street home launched the commercial production of vitamins and drugs in soft gelatin capsule form.

DOWNTOWN • SITES OF INTEREST
ORGANIZED BY PEOPLE MOVER STATIONS

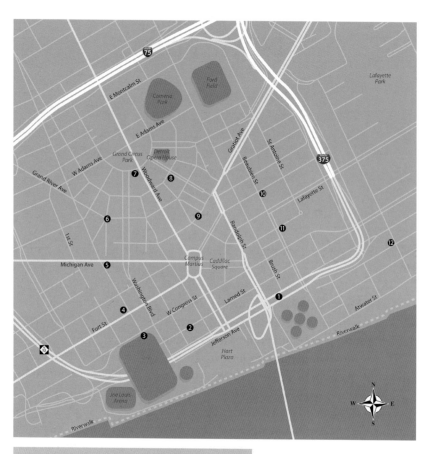

1. **Renaissance / Millender Centers**
2. **Financial District**
3. **Cobo Center**
4. **Fort / Cass**
5. **Michigan Ave**
6. **Times Square**
7. **Grand Circus**
8. **Broadway**
9. **Cadillac Center**
10. **Greektown**
11. **Bricktown**
12. **Outside Central Business District**

CHAPTER 2

DOWNTOWN

For the most part, downtown Detroit is walkable. Sometimes it's much easier to walk the couple blocks to your next destination than ride the Detroit People Mover, an elevated light rail system that loops around the central business district. However, for the clarity and convenience of visitors not familiar with Detroit, downtown sites of historical interest are grouped around pertinent People Mover stations.

The accompanying map should make it easy to navigate the central business district, whether you choose to walk or ride. Please note that each ride on the People Mover costs one token, or seventy-five cents. Tokens can be purchased in each station. Riding the entire route once is recommended, as you not only take in great views of the beautiful Detroit River but also get a better idea of how the downtown area is laid out. Don't forget to take a moment to check out the art installations found in each of the People Mover stations. Brochures providing detailed descriptions of the various works of art can be found on the trains and in each station.

1. RENAISSANCE CENTER/MILLENDER CENTER PEOPLE MOVER STATIONS

Either station provides easy access to Jefferson Avenue, the foot of Woodward (Detroit's main drag) and the waterfront. Here, you'll find an eclectic mix of architecture ranging from the 1840s to the modern towers of the Renaissance Center. You'll also find a collection of mid-century modern buildings built in the 1940s to 1960s as part of the Civic Center redevelopment plan designed to revitalize the downtown area and take advantage of the city's greatest asset: its waterfront. The plan called for the condemnation and clearing of dilapidated and unsightly commercial buildings and docks located along the river between First and Randolph Streets to make way for construction of new, modern buildings.

Buildings constructed as part of this plan included a new city hall, exhibition or convention hall, veterans' memorial building and Ford Auditorium, the latter a new performance center for the Detroit Symphony Orchestra. Built with funds from Ford Motor Company and Ford/Mercury dealer affiliates as a memorial to Henry and Edsel Ford, the auditorium stood on Jefferson just east of Woodward. After the Detroit Symphony Orchestra relocated to the renovated Orchestra Hall, Ford Auditorium sat vacant for many years and met the wrecking ball in 2011.

SAINTS PETER AND PAUL JESUIT CHURCH
438 St. Antoine Street and Jefferson Avenue

The cornerstone of Saints Peter and Paul Jesuit Church is dated June 29, 1844, making it the oldest extant church structure in Detroit. The earliest Jesuit priests arrived in Detroit as part of Cadillac's entourage.

While the exterior is simple in comparison to other local churches, the interior is stunning. The sanctuary is awash in a sea of white, which includes the marble wainscoting, pulpit, communion rail, carved religious statues and exquisite Carrera marble altar designed by Gustave Adolph Mueller.

Tall, arched windows flood the sanctuary with natural light, creating a bright, airy, uplifting space. Unlike many other churches where dark woodwork often overwhelms, the wooden pews, hand-carved confessionals and terra cotta–colored marble floor ground the church instead of competing with the soaring, ethereal expanse. Hand-painted frescoes on the vaulted ceiling and minimal gold accents add a mystical touch to the serene yet inspiring house of worship.

According to church history, Vicar General Peter Kindekens and Francis Latourneau designed the post-classical basilica-style church, which was built by Bishop Peter Paul Lefevere, a French-speaking Belgian. In 1848, it was consecrated as a Catholic cathedral and served in this capacity until 1877, when it was deeded by Bishop Caspar Henry Borgess, Lefevere's

Saints Peter and Paul Jesuit Church was Detroit's first Catholic cathedral. Consecrated in 1848, it's the city's oldest church structure still standing today. *Courtesy of Library of Congress.*

successor, to the Jesuit Order as part of an agreement to start Detroit's first Catholic college. The University of Detroit–Mercy School of Law is still next door.

The church has undergone several renovations since its inception. Original elements dating back to 1848 include the exterior (except for minor modifications), interior frescoes above the high altar painted by local artist Angelo Paldi and the baptismal font.

CHARLES TROMBLY HOUSE
553 East Jefferson Avenue

This three-story brick Italianate town house is one of the city's oldest homes and a rare example of a pre–Civil War extant Detroit residence. It is commonly referred to as the Beaubien House because the property was part of the ribbon farm belonging to descendants of the early French settlers of that name. Ribbon farms were long, narrow parcels of land extending inland several miles from the Detroit River.

Several sources say Charles Trombly purchased the property from his cousin Antoine Beaubien after graduating from Georgetown University and built the home in 1851. The home remained a residential property until the late 1950s, when it was divided into both residential and commercial use. The building served as the offices of the Michigan Architectural Foundation and American Institute of Architects of Michigan. It has been redeveloped as a co-working space.

DuMouchelle Art Gallery
409 East Jefferson Avenue

Fans of *Antiques Roadshow* may be familiar with the DuMouchelle name. Expert appraisers Lawrence, Ernest and Robert DuMouchelle have made frequent appearances on PBS's most-watched ongoing series. Ernest, who served as gallery vice president, passed away in August 2018.

On their PBS bio pages, the gallery is touted as the "Midwest's largest and most prestigious auction house." Founded by Joseph and Charlotte DuMouchelle in 1927, the couple moved their business in 1936 to this former automotive dealership, where it's remained a Detroit fixture ever since. Throngs of people flock to the monthly auctions in search of treasures, and the art gallery is a shopper's paradise.

The six-story brick building itself is historically significant. Per copies of records shared by Robert DuMouchelle, the building department issued a permit to Vinton & Co. in 1902 to construct a two-story brick store on the front of Lot 23 of the Brush farm. The following year, the department issued an alteration permit to Henry B. Joy for construction of the additional four stories. In 1902, the city directory listed "William E. Metzger, Automobiles" as the building occupant. Metzger, who operated one of the largest bicycle shops in the country before becoming enamored with the automobile, is credited with opening the first independent auto dealership in the United States in 1897. The dealership, which sold Waverly Electric Cars, was located across the street where the Renaissance Center stands before he moved his showroom here.

According to the Automotive Hall of Fame, Metzger was one of the automotive industry pioneers responsible for its early growth, especially in Detroit. He helped organize several automobile companies, including Cadillac Motor Car Company, alongside Henry Leland, as well as the nation's first auto show, which debuted right here in Detroit.

The 1906 city directory lists Henry W. Wolcott, a manufacturer's agent for Cadillac Motor Car Company, and Charles Burns, with Automobile Accessory Manufacturing Company, as building tenants.

GM RenCen (Renaissance Center)
400 Renaissance Drive

It's hard to believe that Detroit's most recognizable landmark, an imposing complex of seven interconnected soaring glass and steel towers, has dominated the city's skyline for over forty years. On April 15, 1977, amid much fanfare, a formal dedication was held to commemorate the opening of the seventy-three-story, 727-foot-tall luxury hotel and four surrounding thirty-nine-story towers. Two additional twenty-one-story office towers opened in 1981. When dedicated, the Detroit Plaza Hotel, now a Marriott property, was the tallest all-hotel skyscraper in the world. It held this distinction for nine years until a taller hotel opened in Singapore. It remained the tallest all-hotel skyscraper in the Western Hemisphere until 2014, when a taller Marriott hotel opened in New York.

The vision for the Renaissance Center originated in 1970, when then Ford Motor Company chairman Henry Ford II and other business leaders joined forces to encourage redevelopment in the city. They believed an impressive, large-scale project such as this could breathe new life into the city's dying downtown and jumpstart the local economy. Shortly after the project was announced, a naming contest was held. Renaissance Center was selected from among over 140,000 entries.

City officials embraced the plan, which had private investors such as Ford Motor Company, General Motors and twenty-nine other businesses with ties to the automotive industry and southeast Michigan economy underwriting the estimated $500 million price tag. Several sources claim this was the largest private investment group assembled for an American urban real estate venture. Construction began on May 22, 1973, on thirty-three acres of riverfront property.

Architect John Portman, credited with revitalization projects such as Peachtree Center in Atlanta, Georgia, designed the Renaissance Center as a modern rosette rising from a square podium. According to a 1970s promotional video released by the Renaissance Center Partnership, the 350,000-square-foot podium was designed to house an upscale shopping center.

Other attributes included open soaring spaces with several visible levels incorporating color, light, texture and sound "to touch and delight our senses." The six-story hotel lobby encompassed an acre featuring five levels of suspended pedestrian walkways crossing through it and a reflecting pool with a revolving cocktail island at its center. A 360-degree revolving restaurant crowned the hotel, offering a fresh perspective of the city each minute from seven hundred feet above.

Portman's design reflected his vision of secure internal spaces and a city within a city, both of which would later be criticized as design flaws. While the complex initially garnered excitement, drawing business tenants, high-end retailers and visitors, it wasn't long before this shimmering beauty lost its luster. People viewed the concrete interior as harsh and found the interconnected towers difficult to navigate. The complex appeared isolated from the rest of downtown, and fortress-like concrete structures out front containing the mechanicals made the building even more unwelcoming. The 1987 opening of the Detroit People Mover with a station at the Renaissance Center did little to attract people, as there were few businesses left to pique their interest. Competition from new suburban office complexes resulted in an exodus of business tenants.

The Renaissance Center's future brightened in May 1996 when General Motors purchased it for use as its global headquarters. Multiple sources indicate the undisclosed purchase price was less than $100 million, a fraction of what it cost to build. Over the next eight years, GM would spend $500

An aerial view of the Guardian Building with One Detroit, Renaissance Center and Detroit River in the background. *Courtesy of Library of Congress.*

million on renovations. Navigating the center tower is easy now thanks to a glass circulation ring made up of three hundred etched-glass panels from Japan weighing four hundred pounds each. The Wintergarden, a five-story, fifty-thousand-square-foot atrium, claimed the space of a former parking lot, swimming pool and fitness center and provides public access to the Detroit River, as well as an airy space to dine. GM put out the welcome mat at the front entrance by tearing down the foreboding concrete pyramids that housed outdated technology and installing a front plaza and glass atrium on Jefferson that also serves as a vehicle display. In January 2018, the company unveiled GM World in the center's main exhibit area. Visitors can enjoy changing exhibits where current and historic General Motors models take center stage.

Perhaps the 5.5-million-square-foot Renaissance Center, which is so large, it even has its own zip code, was built ahead of its time—long before the other pieces of Detroit's renaissance would fall into place. Luckily, the visionaries who conceived of this grand project dreamed large and persevered. They weren't concerned with Detroit's past but, rather, with its potential and invested millions of dollars in what they believed would be the architectural achievement of the decade and the catalyst for the city's revival.

The glimmering landmark that has served as a beacon from air, water and land for over forty years is now the bustling hot spot they envisioned. Rather than looking dated and tired, it looks vibrant and fresh as it continues to dominate the skyline, serving as a hub in a new chapter in Detroit's history.

DETROIT RIVERWALK
Runs parallel to Atwood Street and the Detroit River

Heavy industry, parking lots, cement silos and broken concrete sidewalks have given way to a beautiful paved path along the Detroit River that will eventually encompass a nearly six-mile stretch from the Ambassador Bridge to Gabriel Richard Park. Residents and visitors hiking or biking along the RiverWalk will encounter wildflower gardens, sculptures, fountains, a giant sandbox, a marina, Michigan's smallest state park and even a delightful carousel. The Cullen Family Carousel designed by Jeff Briggs features animals native to the area, including an egret, snail, loon, frog, eagle, heron and sturgeon, as well as mythical creatures like the river mermaid and monster instead of traditional horses.

Benches along the route provide comfortable spots to relax or take in scenic views of freighters making their way through the strait. The family-friendly destination is the ideal place to scope out another country. Windsor, the southernmost Canadian city located in the province of Ontario, is directly across the river. Detroiters love to point out that from this unique vantage point, we actually look south to see our neighbor to the north.

Construction is underway to create a sandy beach next to Aretha Franklin Park, formerly Chene Park Amphitheater, a five-thousand-seat outdoor concert venue overlooking the Detroit River.

Pedestrians and cyclists can access the Dequindre Cut from the RiverWalk in front of the Outdoor Adventure Center and across from William G.

Milliken State Park and Harbor. The Dequindre Cut is a two-mile urban greenway that follows a former Grand Truck Railroad line, once a vital part of Detroit's manufacturing history. It connects the East Riverfront, Eastern Market and several residential neighborhoods in between.

PHILIP A. HART PLAZA

1 Hart Plaza (Woodward Avenue and Jefferson Avenue)

This monument-studded, fourteen-acre plaza provides pedestrian access to the Detroit River and is named in honor of the late senator Philip A. Hart, Michigan's forty-ninth lieutenant governor (1955–59), who served with Governor G. Mennen Williams. Elected United States senator in 1959, Hart served in this capacity for three terms. Upon receiving a terminal cancer diagnosis, the senator announced he would not seek reelection to a fourth term in 1976.

The Democratic senator who championed civil rights causes was admired by senators from both parties—so much that they voted unanimously to name the new Senate office building under construction in Washington, D.C., for him. Hart died on December 26, 1976, shortly after the vote took place and a few days before his term would have expired. The Hart Senate Office Building was the first federal building to be named after a living person.

The decorated World War II veteran sustained serious injuries from mortar fire on Utah Beach in Normandy on the first day of the Allied invasion. He earned the Bronze Medal, Invasion Arrowhead and Purple

This vintage postcard depicts the hustle and bustle of the Detroit wharf when steamships were a major mode of transportation and Woodward Avenue extended to the river. *Author's collection.*

Heart for his heroics. His wife, Jane C. Briggs, was the daughter of industrialist and Detroit Tigers owner Walter C. Briggs.

Lake Superior State University offers a scholarship in his name. A biography on the foundation website reads:

In his 18 years as Michigan's Senator, Hart worked tirelessly for passage of the civil rights laws and for measures that would protect consumers from powerful big business interests. He was not known for fiery words or sensational headlines, but was a man held in great esteem by his colleagues—Republican or Democrat, Liberal or Conservative for his moral and ethical standards earning the title "Conscience of the Senate." To him, politics was the noble art of governing and governing was about building a better future for our children and our children's children. Education, the environment, civil rights and economic opportunities for all citizens—these were his causes to build upon for the people of Michigan and the citizens of the United States.

Hart Plaza was the final component of the Civic Center development plan. Dedicated in 1976, it was designed by artist and landscape architect Isamu Noguchi and the architectural firm of Smith, Hinchman & Grylls. At the center of the concrete plaza stands the Horace E. Dodge and Son Memorial Fountain, designed by Noguchi and Walter Budd. *Transcending*, the perpendicular circle rising above a ring of boulders, was gifted to the city by local unions to highlight the labor movement's contributions building the city and creating a middle class. Other monuments and markers of interest include a statue of Detroit founder Antoine de la

Children playing around the Horace E. Dodge and Son Memorial Fountain at Hart Plaza with a picturesque view of Detroit's skyline. *Rod Arroyo.*

31

Mothe Cadillac, a heroic-sized bust of Abraham Lincoln by Gutzon Borglum, a marker denoting the site where Ford Motor Company articles of incorporation were drawn and the Gateway to Freedom International Monument by Ed Dwight commemorating the city and state's participation in the Underground Railroad.

Many major annual events are held at Hart Plaza, including Motor City Pride, Michigan's largest LGBTQ pride celebration in June; Movement Electronic Music Festival, an annual three-day event held over Memorial Day weekend celebrating Detroit's electronic music legacy; and Detroit Jazz Festival, one of the world's premier jazz festivals, held over Labor Day weekend since 1980. The latter free festival features name acts and spills out over several blocks.

DETROIT-WINDSOR TUNNEL
100 East Jefferson Avenue

On November 1, 1939, when the Detroit-Windsor Tunnel was officially dedicated, President Herbert Hoover turned a gold key in Washington, D.C., and bells rang in both Windsor and Detroit to mark its opening. Completed at a cost of $23 million and one year early, the tunnel is still considered an engineering marvel and remains the only international underwater border crossing where one drives his or her own vehicle through.

Approximately twelve thousand cars pass daily through the one-mile tunnel located 75 feet below the surface of the Detroit River and jointly owned by the cities of Detroit and Windsor. No need to worry about lack of air if you're stuck below in traffic, as a sophisticated filtration system pumps 1.5 million cubic feet of fresh air into the tunnel every minute.

Construction of the river section of the tunnel was the most spectacular part of the operation, according to the Detroit-Windsor Tunnel website. It involved sinking nine steel tubes into a trench dug across the bottom of the river.

The steel shells were built on dry land, welded watertight, sealed and floated into the river. Once they were tugged and anchored into position of the trench, the final interior and exterior concrete was poured, and the tubes were sunk and joined together by divers using a collar of tremie cement. Once the tube was in place, the trench was backfilled with 20 feet of material to hold it in place. Meanwhile, the crews drove the shield section

This vintage postcard highlights Detroit's waterfront skyline and its proximity to Windsor, Ontario, via the tunnel or "Fleetway," a four-minute drive from Detroit to Windsor. *Author's collection.*

toward the tube, traveling underground 466 feet on the U.S. side and 986 feet on the Canadian side, changing courses both vertically and horizontally. When contact with the submerged tube was made, there was less than one-inch error in alignment.

Visitors can experience history by driving through our nation's second-busiest international border crossing, which underwent a $50 million renovation in 1993. Another renovation is underway. Don't forget your passport or other forms of accepted documentation!

MARINERS' CHURCH
170 East Jefferson Avenue

Mariners' Church was established in 1842 when Julia Anderson, a widow, bequeathed the property where her mansion stood at the corner of Woodward Avenue and Woodbridge Street (now Hart Plaza) to be used to build a stone church with "forever free" pews, according to church history.

After the Erie Canal opened in 1825, Detroit became a bustling port city. Anderson and her sister, Charlotte Taylor, noticed how sailors were looked down upon by society and relegated to the back pews in local churches. They envisioned creating a more inclusive church that would be free of class constraints.

The autonomous Anglican church is unique because it's not affiliated with any diocese, and it's the only Michigan church incorporated by an act of the Michigan legislature. In its early days, the church survived financially by leasing out first-floor retail space to local merchants.

The church, which may have served as a safe house on the Underground Railroad, became famous when singer/songwriter Gordon Lightfoot mentioned it in his ballad "The Wreck of the *Edmund Fitzgerald*." He immortalized the ringing of the church bell twenty-nine times in memory of each crew member who died aboard the iron ore carrier when it sank in Lake Superior in November 1975. Incidentally, the *Edmund Fitzgerald* was built at Great Lakes Engineering Works, once located in the nearby suburb of Ecorse, and was launched from neighboring city River Rouge on June 8, 1958. At 729 feet and 13,632 gross tons, it was the largest ship on the Great Lakes for thirteen years, until 1971, according to information found on the Shipwreck Museum at Whitefish Bay's website.

Old Mariners' Church, originally slated for demolition in the 1950s to make way for the new Civic Center development, stands in contrast to the modern buildings. *Rod Arroyo.*

Consecrated in 1849, Mariners' Church nearly met the wrecking ball in 1955 to make way for the Civic Center development. Instead, the three-thousand-ton church was moved nine hundred feet east to its current location.

While the church is open to all, it remains true to its maritime roots by incorporating newer traditions, such as officiating over the annual Blessing of the Fleet and the Great Lakes Memorial Service. Visitors are encouraged to attend weekly services to view the beautiful stained-glass windows that depict scenes from the Bible and celebrate the city's seafaring roots and other noteworthy architectural features.

UAW-FORD NATIONAL PROGRAMS CENTER
151 West Jefferson Avenue

The beautiful ten-story marble UAW-Ford National Programs Center is still referred to by many locals as the Veterans Memorial Building. UAW-Ford purchased the building from the city in 2014 after leasing it as a training center for twenty years. Special building features include a large main-floor theater-style conference room and a two-hundred-seat lecture hall.

The building is significant for several reasons. It marks the founding of present-day Detroit. It's believed Antoine de la Mothe Cadillac came ashore where the building now stands on July 24, 1701, and established the trading post settlement of Fort Pontchartrain du Detroit. A historic marker denoting the region's first French settlement can be found across the street on the front façade of the Crown Plaza Hotel.

A vintage postcard of the Veterans' Memorial Building, the first building completed as part of the Civic Center development project. The victory eagle is a carved relief by sculptor Marshall Fredericks. *Author's collection.*

An artist's depiction of French explorer and Detroit founder Antoine de la Mothe Cadillac greeting his wife, Madame Marie-Therese Guyon Cadillac. *Courtesy of Library of Congress.*

In 1921, city officials designated the site to be used as a memorial to American casualties of the Spanish-American and First World Wars. The idea of a memorial finally came to fruition following World War II, and Veterans Memorial Building was officially dedicated on June 11, 1950. The Memorial was the first structure built as part of the new Civic Center development.

The victory eagle prominently positioned on the front of the building is the work of Marshall M. Fredericks, a local sculptor considered one of the most prolific of the twentieth century. He's known worldwide for his figurative sculpture, public memorials, fountains, portraits and animals. The Marshall M. Fredericks Sculpture Museum digital archives describe the eagle as measuring thirty feet tall and projecting four and a half feet from the wall. The nearby *Spirit of Detroit* statue in front of city hall is also a Fredericks commission.

A life-size bronze monument inside the lobby pays tribute to UAW president Walter P. Reuther and Ford Motor Company CEO Henry Ford II. Artist Richard Miller depicted the two men shaking hands across the bargaining table, symbolizing a spirit of cooperation between labor and management.

In May 1970, Reuther and his wife, May, lay in repose inside the building. The couple and four others had died earlier that month in a tragic airplane accident at Pellston Regional Airport, located in northern Michigan, twenty-five miles from the United Auto Workers' Black Lake retreat. The crash occurred as the pilot tried to land during heavy rain and fog. Other casualties included Mrs. Reuther's nephew William Wolfman, who served as the couple's bodyguard; renowned Philadelphia architect and family friend Oscar Stonorov; and pilots George Evans and Joseph Karrafa.

MONUMENT TO JOE LOUIS
Intersection of Woodward and Jefferson Avenues

This tribute to boxing legend Joe Louis—still considered one of the greatest heavyweight champions of all time—by sculptor Robert Graham stands prominently in the island of one of Detroit's busiest intersections. A gift to the city by *Sports Illustrated* magazine in 1986, the massive eight-thousand-pound bronze sculpture features a twenty-four-foot-long forearm and fist suspended from a pyramidal support of bronze poles and stands twenty-four feet tall.

The Joe Louis fist statue and towering GM Renaissance Center are two iconic landmarks. Mariners' Church and the entrance to the Detroit/Windsor Tunnel are also pictured. *Rod Arroyo.*

Born into poverty on May 13, 1914, in Alabama, Joe Louis Barrow was the seventh of eight children born to Munroe and Lillie Barrow. His father, a sharecropper, was committed to an asylum when Louis was only two years old. Not long after hearing of her husband's death, Lillie remarried and moved the family to Detroit in hopes of escaping the discrimination black families faced in the South.

To keep her son out of trouble, Lillie enrolled him in violin lessons. Instead, he used this money to train as a boxer at the Brewster Recreation Center and fought under the name "Joe Louis" so his mother wouldn't find out. Louis turned pro in 1934 after winning fifty out of fifty-four amateur bouts.

Louis won his first twenty-seven professional fights, which included victories against former heavyweight champions Primo Carnera and Max Baer. His winning streak came to an end on June 19, 1936, at the hands of German boxer Max Schmeling, who was considered the underdog. Louis was crushed. Several news accounts included reports of Louis crying in his dressing room afterward.

Louis would go on to usurp heavyweight champion James Braddock and capture this coveted title the following year. Despite this huge victory, Louis still seethed over what he called his embarrassing loss to Schmeling the previous year.

On June 22, 1938, Louis got his opportunity to exact revenge on Schmeling at Yankee Stadium before a crowd of over seventy thousand attendees. The fight was broadcast over the radio as millions of listeners around the world tuned in.

The fight was more than a Louis-Schmeling rematch. To many, it symbolized democracy versus fascism. Adolph Hitler's Nazi regime was on the rise, and World War II would break out in Europe the following year. Anti-German sentiment ran high. Ironically, Louis, who represented democracy, didn't enjoy the same rights as white men in his own country. And Schmeling never pledged allegiance to the Nazi Party. In a fight lasting just over two minutes, democracy prevailed, and the Brown Bomber catapulted color barriers and became the nation's first black national hero.

The years between 1937 and 1949 would be known as Louis's "reign of terror" as he successfully defended his title many times. When the United States entered World War II, Louis enlisted in the army. He fought in nearly one hundred exhibitions before military audiences and donated the prize money to the military relief fund. He became a spokesperson for army recruiting and used his appeal to encourage the enlistment of African Americans.

When Louis retired in 1949, he was the undefeated world champion. His retirement was short-lived, however. Financial pressures from an extravagant and generous lifestyle along with IRS debts forced him back into the ring far past his prime, and he experienced several defeats. According to his biography on the official Joe Louis website, "Louis earned $5 million during his boxing career. At age 37, he didn't have a 'single cent' to show for it." Plagued with financial woes, Louis was able to parlay his celebrity status and work as a greeter at Caesar's Palace casino in Las Vegas, a position he held from 1970 until his death in 1981 from a heart attack.

At President Ronald Reagan's request, Louis received a hero's burial, complete with military honors, at Arlington National Cemetery. Max

The historic June 1938 rematch between heavyweight champions Joe Louis and Max Schmeling. Louis's victory represented a win for democracy over fascism and propelled him to national hero status. *Courtesy of Library of Congress.*

Schmeling not only served as a pallbearer at the funeral but paid for some of the burial expenses.

"The Fist," as the monument is commonly referred to, was not without detractors when unveiled. Some people thought the disembodied arm didn't do the prizefighter justice and preferred a literal interpretation or at least the inclusion of a boxing glove (a full-bodied statue of the Brown Bomber can be found inside Cobo Center). Many critics thought the clenched fist glorified violence or paid homage to the black power movement. Some didn't think the monument aptly conveyed Louis's generous nature or his grace. For example, Louis may have cried after his first defeat by Schmeling, but with victory he was a gracious winner and never gloated.

Graham, who died in 2008, seemed pleased by the attention and strong reactions to his second major public work. Carol Young, appointed by then mayor Coleman A. Young to oversee the project, responded to the criticism in a 1986 *Los Angeles Times* article by saying Detroit officials were happy with the comments. "It would have been too bad if people yawned and walked by."

People certainly don't yawn today when walking by this iconic memorial. It's rather common to see tourists climb up on the platform, extend their forearms and clenched fists and pose for photographs to document their visit to the Motor City.

SPIRIT OF DETROIT / COLEMAN A. YOUNG MUNICIPAL CENTER
2 Woodward Avenue

The *Spirit of Detroit* statue located at the front entrance of the Coleman A. Young Municipal Center is one of the most recognized Detroit landmarks and a popular photo stop. The bronze statue cast in Oslo, Norway, was designed by Michigan artist Marshall Fredericks. It sits atop a Vermont marble base and cost $58,000. It's been reported Fredericks waived his fee, citing civic duty, and even paid for some expenses himself. When installed in 1958, the statue was the largest bronze sculpture cast since the Renaissance. The sculpture features a man in the kneeling position holding a sphere emanating rays of light in his left hand that is supposed to represent the Deity. In his right hand he holds a man, woman and child.

A *Detroit Free Press* article dated April 21, 1958, describes how the nine-ton statue arrived at 6:55 a.m. that morning from Oslo via Cleveland aboard the German ship *Thomas Schulte*.

The twenty-six-foot-tall bronze *Spirit of Detroit* sculpture by Marshall Fredericks is an iconic Detroit landmark. *Rod Arroyo.*

When the artist unveiled plans for the sculpture in April 1955, the *Detroit Free Press* reported the twenty-one-foot-wide and fourteen-foot-tall art piece would "represent the spirit of man as the noblest expression of God." Fredericks told reporters his design was made to conform as nearly as possible to the inscription on the symbol wall located behind the statue that reads: "And the Lord is that spirit, and where the spirit of the Lord is, there is liberty." While Fredericks didn't name the statue, it's believed the *Spirit of Detroit* came about because of this inscription. It could also be attributed to newspaper articles at the time, such as this *Detroit Free Press* headline: "Can't Deny Detroit Has Spirit."

The statue is synonymous with Detroit and is often seen in video clips and movies filmed in the city. The image is used as the City of Detroit's official logo. When Detroit's professional sports teams are in the playoffs, the *Spirit* is dressed up in oversized versions of their team jerseys. In 2007, the statue underwent an extensive renovation to prepare for its fiftieth birthday the following year. In early 2018, the statue was gussied up for its sixtieth birthday.

Behind the forty-foot marble curtain serving as the backdrop to the *Spirit of Detroit* is the entrance to the Coleman A. Young Municipal Center. Completed in 1955 as the City County Building, this modern structure designed in the International style by architects Harley, Ellington and Day serves as government offices for both the City of Detroit and Wayne County. It replaced the former Detroit City Hall, which was located across from Campus Martius and has since been demolished, and the Wayne County Building, which is located on Randolph Street.

The building consists of two towers. The twenty-story court tower is occupied by Wayne County Probate and Third Circuit Courts. Administrative offices for the City of Detroit—including the mayor's office and city council chambers and some Wayne County offices such as the Wayne County Clerk—are located in the fourteen-story tower. If you need a marriage license or business permit, this is the place to go.

Mayor Coleman Alexander Young was elected Detroit's first African American mayor in 1973. The former civil rights activist, union organizer and Michigan senator served an unprecedented five terms as mayor. He died of respiratory failure at the age of seventy-nine on November 29, 1997. The building was renamed in his honor after his death.

CAMPUS MARTIUS PARK/CADILLAC SQUARE
800 Woodward Avenue

Located in the heart of the business district, both Campus Martius and Cadillac Square are easily accessible from several People Mover stations and other points of interest. Because tourists regularly walk the three-block distance from the corner of Woodward and Jefferson Avenues to these sites, we're including them here and referencing several buildings found along the way.

Walking along Woodward Avenue north of Congress Street, you'll notice several structures on the east side of the street that date back to the late nineteenth century. The 1879 building occupied by Grand Trunk Pub once housed Traub Bros. & Company jewelry store, followed by a Grand Trunk ticket office. Mabley and Company department store occupied the large black-and-white painted building north of the pub before becoming the sixty-room Metropole Hotel.

Three buildings in this block were designed by celebrated Detroit architect Albert Kahn or his firm, two of which bookend the nineteenth-century buildings mentioned in the preceding paragraph. The twelve-story, Romanesque-inspired Vinton Building opened in 1917. The unique design of the twenty-six-story Neoclassical First National Building, located at 660 Woodward Avenue, zigzags through the middle of the block and features a Corinthian portico with eighteen columns spanning the Woodward Avenue and Cadillac Square elevations. Completed in 1922, it was built for First National Bank, established one year after the passage of the National Banking Act. Directly across the street, the modern Chase building opened

Looking north on Woodward from Jefferson, the First National Building looms in back. Visible businesses include Avenue Burlesque, Peerless Painless Dentists, Lincoln Bond and Mortgage Company. An early traffic signal, another Detroit first, stands to the right. *Courtesy of Library of Congress.*

in 1959 and features a checkerboard curtain wall pattern composed of Georgia Cherokee marble.

Campus Martius has long played a role as a gathering place in Detroit's history. Its name is Latin for "field of Mars," fitting for a military parade or exercise ground located inside or near a city such as Rome. During Detroit's early days as a military outpost, militias drilled here. Soldier recruiting events and troop sendoff ceremonies took place here during the Civil War years. When President Abraham Lincoln was assassinated in April 1865, residents assembled in the park to pay their respects at the public eulogy.

A circular marker in front of Parc restaurant denotes Detroit's point of origin, as dictated by Judge Augustus B. Woodward's elaborate plan to rebuild Detroit following its destruction by fire in 1805. Inspired by Pierre Charles L'Enfant's 1791 master plan to transform Washington, D.C., into a grand capital with wide garden-lined avenues, public squares and inspiring buildings, the Woodward Plan called for 200-foot-wide north–south and east–west boulevards intersected by circular plazas or circuses. Like spokes on a wheel, 120-foot-wide secondary avenues would radiate from the circuses, with a network of smaller streets linking two

A modern lobby re-do of the historic First National Building, a twenty-six-floor commercial building designed by Albert Kahn. It opened in 1922. *Rod Arroyo.*

"The Heart of Detroit," a vintage photo of Campus Martius and Cadillac Square, shows the tower of Detroit's old city hall (demolished) in the foreground with old Wayne County Courthouse in the distance. *Courtesy of Library of Congress.*

boulevards and four avenues. The resulting hexagonal units could be repeated and connected, enabling the city to expand in any direction to meet population growth. Public buildings, churches and schools would occupy the grand circuses.

This complex plan was nixed in 1808 for a variety of reasons, including the location of Fort Shelby, which prevented its extension to the south, and property owners weren't keen on relinquishing part of their land. *All*

Our Yesterdays: A Brief History of Detroit authors Frank and Arthur Woodford describe still-visible implementations of the plan: "Campus Martius, which marked a corner of the original hexagon, is one of the open plazas with streets like Woodward, Michigan, Cadillac Square, Fort, and Monroe radiating from it." Nearby Grand Circus Park is another dramatic example of half of one of Woodward's projected circuses or large open spaces, and his radiating boulevards and avenues (Washington and Madison) are clearly discernable.

Today, the park serves as a popular gathering place for downtown dwellers, employees and visitors. Warm-weather months find guests enjoying sponsored outdoor movies and concerts or just relaxing amid the pleasant views of the Woodward Fountain and Michigan Soldiers and Sailors Monument. The beautiful Randolph Rogers tribute to Michigan soldiers who died in the Civil War is one of the city's oldest pieces of public art. Campus Martius turns into a winter wonderland during colder months with the installation of the much-anticipated annual Christmas tree and outdoor ice rink.

During the nineteenth century, Cadillac Square was the site of the bustling Central Market, where locals purchased meat and produce from vendors hawking their wares, and, later, a busy bus terminal for a large part of the twentieth century. Today, it's an extension of Campus Martius and is kept active with rotating food trucks, seasonal markets and other events.

The Bagley Memorial Fountain, gifted to the city in 1886 by the estate of John Judson Bagley, Michigan's sixteenth governor, has been moved several

Looking downward to Cadillac Square, a popular public gathering space. Bagley Memorial Fountain, found on right, is the only remaining local work by architect Henry Hobson Richardson. *Courtesy of Bedrock.*

times and now stands in the square. The city's first public drinking fountain was designed by Henry Hobson Richardson and is the only known Michigan work still surviving by this noted architect. The governor wanted Detroiters to always enjoy fresh running water.

The Old Wayne County Court House borders the east end of Cadillac Square and is considered one of the most significant courthouses in Michigan. This beautiful example of Beaux Arts–style architecture opened in 1902 and was immediately deemed old-fashioned, as people wanted modern buildings. It housed county courts and other administrative offices until county executives purchased the nearby Guardian Building. The John Scott–designed building is privately owned and sits vacant, with no news of development plans at this time.

Other significant buildings bordering these public gathering spaces include One Campus Martius (Meridian) and the National Theatre. One Campus Martius, an award-winning office building built as the headquarters for Compuware, opened in 2003 and features a delightful kite sculpture fountain designed by WET Design, the same firm that designed the famous Dubai and Bellagio fountains. The fifteen colorful glass kites suspended at more than fourteen stories tall represented the largest indoor hanging water feature in the world when first built. Incidentally, the fountain at Campus Martius Park is also by WET Design.

Visitors always inquire about the stunning and unusual National Theatre located at 16 Monroe Street. Designed by Albert Kahn and Ernest Wilby, this final vestige of Detroit's first theater district opened in 1911. Even in

This view captures the Shepherd Fairey mural on the former Compuware headquarters, the Penobscot Building peeking over the top and the Art Deco–style David Stott Building in the distance. The vacant lot in front is the site of the former J.L. Hudson department store and is currently under redevelopment. *Courtesy of Bedrock.*

A vintage postcard depicts a bird's-eye view of Detroit from the old city hall tower. The green space is Cadillac Square, with Wayne County Courthouse at the end. *Author's collection.*

Victory and *Progress*, two stunning chariot sculptures, flank the center tower of the old Wayne County Building, an architectural gem constructed in the Beaux Arts style. *Rod Arroyo.*

its forlorn state, one can appreciate the beauty of this twin-tower, glazed terra cotta movie house infused with colorful Pewabic tiles and a recessed front arch. *AIA Detroit* authors Eric J. Hill and John Gallagher describe its design as hybrid Baroque, Beaux Arts and Moorish amusement park style. Unless preservationists prevail in their push to save the entire building, recently released renderings show only the ornate façade incorporated as a gateway to a new development.

2. FINANCIAL DISTRICT PEOPLE MOVER STATION

This station provides easy access to the Financial District, a designated historic district that pays homage to what was once the financial heart of the city from the 1850s to the 1970s. Here you'll find great examples of architecture that coincide with the city's financial upturns and development. The area was also home to Detroit's first stock exchange. Financial institutions continue to be an important part of the district.

ONE WOODWARD
1 Woodward Avenue

This beautiful example of mid-century modern architecture draws admirers of this style from all over the world. The twenty-eight-story headquarters built for Michigan Consolidated Gas, the largest and oldest utility in the state at the time, opened in 1962 and was designed by Minoru Yamasaki. Yamasaki would later design the World Trade Center Twin Towers destroyed by terrorists in 2001. Yamasaki resided in metro Detroit, and several of his works can be found in Detroit and the suburbs. One Woodward was his first skyscraper commission, and many of the design elements incorporated here were replicated in the Twin Towers.

The Minoru Yamasaki–designed Michigan Consolidated Gas Company headquarters now known as One Woodward, seen through *Transcending*, a monument dedicated to the labor movement. *Courtesy of Bedrock.*

GUARDIAN BUILDING
500 Griswold Avenue

Without fail, this Art Deco masterpiece, considered by many to be Detroit's most beautiful building, evokes awe in first-time visitors. Some even assert it's the finest example of Art Deco architecture in the entire world. The building earned its nickname "cathedral to finance" when it opened in 1929 because the banking hall's soaring five-story vaulted ceiling gives the illusion of a house of worship. Today, one can almost hear monks chanting in reverence to the almighty dollar.

Detroit was a boomtown in the 1920s, and money was plentiful. The Union Trust Company, which became part of the Guardian Detroit Union Group holding company after several mergers, held 40 percent of the region's assets. Board members wanted to construct a new headquarters that suitably reflected their stature. Wirt C. Rowland, an architect for Smith, Hinchman & Grylls, received carte blanche to design such a building, which he did at a cost of $12 million.

The Guardian's exterior incorporates fine brickwork on a red granite base, a repeating theme of stepped arches and colorful terra cotta accents at the windows and setbacks that draw the eye upward to the forty-story north tower. His design called for the nearly two million bricks used in construction to be colored a specific shade of orange dubbed "Guardian brick." Two large figural reliefs designed by Corrado Parducci flank the main entrance and represent safety and security. Above the entrance, the semicircular dome made of Pewabic tiles, Detroit's contribution to the Arts and Crafts movement, features a likeness of an aviator symbolizing progress.

The banking hall of the Guardian Building, aptly dubbed the "cathedral to finance." Because of strong Native American influences, the design is often referred to as Aztec Deco. *Rod Arroyo.*

49

The impressive lobby contains dramatic stepped or notched arches over the entrance and elevator corridors and vibrant Rookwood Pottery tiles arranged in a stunning diamond pattern on the ceiling. The notched arch motif repeats itself throughout the building in marble floor patterns and decorative elements embellishing elevator doors, doorknobs, drinking fountains and more.

A rare Tiffany clock embedded in the ornamental Monel metal grille separates the lobby and lavish banking hall. An epic allegorical mural of Michigan by Ezra A. Winter spans the south wall and depicts dominant industries in the state at the time. The prominent early twentieth-century muralist and Michigan native's best-known works are the *Canterbury Tales* inside the Library of Congress and *Fountain of Youth* in Radio City Music Hall's foyer. Winter also designed the inlaid mosaic containing the Union Trust's creed found in the lobby above the security desk. A spectacular stenciled canvas ceiling treatment by the Thomas DiLorenzo Company of New York features colorful geometric patterns resembling Native American designs. It's backed with horsehair to provide the cavernous hall with optimum acoustics.

The view from One Campus Martius of the Guardian Building, Detroit's Art Deco jewel, situated between two modern structures built during the Civic Center development project. *Courtesy of Bedrock.*

The stock market crashed shortly after the Guardian opened, and the nation plunged into a severe economic downturn known as the Great Depression. Detroit's economy, closely tied to automotive manufacturing, plummeted. The Guardian Building is significant for its association with this major episode of American history, notes the City of Detroit publication *The Proposed Historic Detroit Financial District Final Report.* The Guardian Detroit Union Group—composed of several local financial institutions, including the Union Trust Company—continued to disperse its normal dividends to shareholders despite the worsening conditions of its member banks. Federal and state examiners declared it insolvent, prompting Michigan governor William A. Comstock to close all state banks on

The lobby of the Guardian Building, an Art Deco jewel considered by many to be
Detroit's most beautiful building and the finest example of this type of architecture in the
world. *Rod Arroyo.*

February 24, 1933, to avoid bank runs, or mass customer withdrawals, while examiners investigated. This forced "bank holiday" was only to last eight days but remained in effect longer.

The Union Trust's insolvency led directly to Michigan's banking crash and a nationwide crisis of confidence that closed banks in most states prior to President Roosevelt declaring a federal "bank holiday" on March 6, 1933, two days after his inauguration.

During World War II, the Guardian and Buhl Buildings served as command centers for administrators who oversaw the production and distribution of military goods.

Ownership of the Guardian has changed several times over the years. Today, it's the seat of Wayne County government and is occupied by other professional tenants.

PENOBSCOT BUILDING

645 Griswold Street

This forty-seven-story office tower reigned as the tallest building in Michigan until the construction of the Renaissance Center in the 1970s. Now, it's the city's third-tallest building. The Penobscot Building spans an entire block and was constructed in three phases, with the tallest section being the most recognizable. When this portion was completed in early 1928, it was the tallest building outside New York and Chicago.

Named for a Native American tribe from Maine, the Art Deco limestone-clad building was designed by Wirt C. Rowland for the Simon J. Murphy Company. Maine was the birthplace of the company's founder, who made his fortune in the lumber trade.

Interior and exterior ornamentation includes reliefs symbolic to Native Americans, such as birds, beasts and warriors, and a frieze representing a treaty between white settlers and Native Americans. Emblematic figures depicting commerce, industry and prosperity can be found on the ornate bronze elevator doors and elsewhere throughout the building.

For several decades, a rooftop observation deck provided sightseers with sweeping views of the city. The swanky penthouse Penobscot Club called the "nightclub in the sky" offered stunning views and lively nightlife.

A flaming beacon measuring twelve feet in diameter and soaring over six hundred feet above street level has long been an identifying feature of this landmark. In an advertisement commemorating the Penobscot opening,

This vintage photograph represents four different architectural eras and styles. *Left to right*: Chase Tower, also called The Qube, 1959; Penobscot Building, 1928; Dime Building, 1912; old city hall, 1871 (demolished in 1961). *Courtesy of Library of Congress.*

manufacturer Bellows-Claude Neon Tubelites described the "ball of fire" as a guidepost of the aerial age and said that it "marks the city from the air more than fifty miles away on a clear night and flyers will tell you that by it alone can they find Detroit through the mists."

The Penobscot Building has been occupied by many legal tenants over the years. In 1991, the State Bar of Michigan and Detroit Bar Association dedicated and placed a historic marker inside the building's lobby called *The Uninvited Ear*. The marker commemorates Federal District Court judge Damon Keith's 1971 decision upholding the right of Americans to be free from government intrusion.

When the U.S. Department of Justice was challenged after wiretapping conversations involving a suspect in the bombing of a CIA office in Ann Arbor, Michigan, without first obtaining judicial approval, the department argued the attorney general could order wiretaps in cases concerning domestic national security without prior judicial approval. Judge Keith rejected that argument, citing the Fourth Amendment protection of "a defendant from the evil of the uninvited ear."

FORD BUILDING
615 Griswold Street

Designed by Daniel Burnham and Company, this Neoclassic, eighteen-story, white terra cotta high-rise is one of three remaining buildings in

Detroit designed by the noted architect. Considered the preeminent architect of the late nineteenth century, Burnham is regarded as the "father of modern planning." His significant design contributions include the 1893 World's Columbian Exposition in Chicago, Plan of Chicago of 1909 and New York's Flatiron Building.

Construction of the Ford Building began in 1907 and was completed in 1909, making it one of the oldest skyscrapers in the city. It was also one of the first buildings in Detroit to utilize a steel frame, and for many years, it was the city's tallest building.

The Ford namesake behind this building was Toledo-based glass manufacturer Edward Ford.

During the 1926 Ossian Sweet trials, famed trial lawyer Clarence Darrow led the defense from offices on the seventeenth floor. (See Frank Murphy Hall of Justice for more information).

Buhl Building
535 Griswold Street

Designed by Wirt C. Rowland, this twenty-nine-story Neo-Gothic high-rise opened in 1925. The Buhl family settled in Detroit during the early nineteenth century and found their fortune in furs and hats. Later generations became involved in locomotive manufacturing and ironworks.

Aerial views reveal the building's cross formation, a design used to maximize natural light and breezes since air conditioning and electricity were still in their infancy. Architectural sculptural elements by master craftsman Corrado Parducci, a mosaic tiled entry and ornate ceilings are just a few details that make this building stand out.

Early maps indicate the southeast portion of Fort Shelby extended to where the Buhl Building now stands. The military fort built by the British in 1779 was originally called Fort Lernoult. American general William Hull surrendered the fort to the British during the War of 1812 until American troops reclaimed it in 1813. So for a brief time, Detroit was back under British control. The fort was demolished in 1827, and a historic marker is located nearby at the corner of Fort and Shelby Streets.

DIME BUILDING/CHRYSLER HOUSE
719 Griswold Street

Light and white define this Neoclassic beauty, designed by famed architect Daniel Burnham. The twenty-three-story office tower is designed in a U shape, enabling natural light to flood the light court above the grand lobby. Tall Corinthian columns in the lobby set the tone for this elegant and classic building.

Left: Daniel Burnham, preeminent architect of the early twentieth century, brought Neoclassical architecture to Detroit with his design of the Dime Building, now called Chrysler House. *Rod Arroyo.*

Below: This safe inside the former Dime Savings Bank headquarters now serves as a conference room for the dPOP interior design studio. *Courtesy of Bedrock.*

Now called Chrysler House, it was originally built for the Dime Savings Bank, so named because one only needed a dime to open an account. The offices for the Lincoln Highway Association—the transcontinental highway running from New York to San Francisco—were located on the top floor. Although the highway doesn't cross through Michigan, members of the association instrumental in the highway's construction, such as Henry B. Joy, lived in Detroit.

3. COBO CENTER PEOPLE MOVER STATION

COBO CENTER
1 Washington Boulevard

Cobo Center is situated on the banks of the Detroit River near where Antoine de la Mothe Cadillac and his entourage first stepped ashore and established the French settlement now known as Detroit. Formerly called Cobo Hall, it opened in 1960 and served as the centerpiece of the Civic Center development project. Named after Albert E. Cobo, Detroit's mayor from 1950 to 1957, and designed by architect Gino Rossetti of Giffels and Vallet, Cobo Hall was one of the first larger convention centers in the nation. One of the premier events held here every January is the North American International Auto Show, which draws press and visitors from all over the world. As of 2020, the auto show will be held in June.

Cobo Arena was once home to the NBA professional basketball team Detroit Pistons and host to a variety of popular events, such as wrestling, circuses and concerts, including those by popular rock legends such as The Who, Led Zeppelin and Aerosmith.

On June 23, 1963, the Detroit "Walk to Freedom" took place on Woodward Avenue, attracting over 125,000 participants, with some accounts stating 250,000. It was led by the late civil rights icon Reverend Dr. Martin Luther King Jr., who called the Sunday afternoon march "the largest and greatest demonstration for freedom ever held in the United States."

The march ended at Cobo Hall, where Dr. King first debuted his "I Have a Dream" speech inside the arena before a capacity crowd estimated at twenty-five thousand—two months prior to his delivery of this historic speech in Washington, D.C. Both speeches were recorded on the Motown record label.

A modern view of the Detroit skyline from across the Detroit River featuring the newly renovated Cobo Center, home of the annual North American International Auto Show. *Courtesy of Cobo Center.*

In the Detroit speech, King invoked the familiar refrain "I have a dream this afternoon, that one day" to reference nearly a dozen different situations, such as one day when the sons of former slaves and slave owners would live together in harmony, black and white children would join hands as brothers and sisters and his own four children would be judged on the content of their character and not the color of their skin. One reference specifically addressed Detroit's discriminatory real estate laws: "I have a dream this afternoon that one day, right here in Detroit, Negroes will be able to buy a house or rent a house anywhere that their money will carry them."

The speech concluded with these memorable words: "With this speed, we'll be able to achieve this new day when all of God's children, black men and white men, Jews and Gentiles, Protestants and Catholics, will be able to join hands and sing with the Negroes in the spiritual of old, 'free at last, free at last.'"

A historic plaque affixed to the building's northeast entrance near Larned Street marks the nearby birthplace of circus entrepreneur James A. McGinnis, who adopted the name "Bailey" after joining the circus at age fourteen. While the "greatest showman" P.T. Barnum garnered all the fame and glory, his quiet partner James A. Bailey ran the show. Born on July 4, 1847, his marker reads:

> *Developing a striking talent for advertising and management, he bought the Cooper & Bailey Shows which toured, under canvas, the world over. Further success came with Bailey's 1880 purchase of "Little America," the first elephant born in this country. The native Detroiter*

J.A. Bailey, the other half of famous circus partnership Barnum and Bailey, was born in Detroit. A historic marker at Cobo Center denotes his birthplace. *Courtesy of Library of Congress.*

joined forces with celebrated showman Phineas T. Barnum in 1881. Overshadowed by his more flamboyant partner, Bailey guided the circus to many triumphs. Unlike Barnum who asserted, "The public likes to be humbugged," Bailey said, "Give the people the best…and they'll reward you." Barnum died in 1891, and Bailey ran the mammoth three-ring show until his death in 1906.

After Bailey's death, Ringling Brothers acquired the circus. The Ringling Brothers and Barnum & Bailey Circus continued until the last show in Uniondale, New York, on May 21, 2017.

The Atwater Street entrance provides access to the Detroit River. The Carl Milles sculpture of a Native American carrying a canoe installed here honors indigenous people and the river's role as a major transportation route. Nearby, a new fresco titled *Detroit: Crossroad of Innovation* by Hubert Massey, who studied under an assistant to Diego Rivera, has been completed. This thirty- by thirty-foot work utilizes the age-old, time-consuming technique of painting on wet plaster.

Hockey fans may want to disembark at the next People Mover station for a final look at Joe Louis Arena, home to the Detroit Red Wings since 1979, before it's demolished to make way for commercial development. The team played its final game at "The Joe" on April 9, 2017, amid much fanfare and left on a high note with a 4–1 win over the New Jersey Devils. Little Caesars Arena is the team's new home. This station provides easy access to the RiverWalk.

4. FORT/CASS PEOPLE MOVER STATION

This People Mover station is located in a once upscale late nineteenth-century residential neighborhood. Prominent residents included United States senator Zachariah Chandler, Michigan governor Russell Alger and wealthy landowner Lewis Cass, second governor of the Michigan Territory and twenty-second United States secretary of state. Fort Street Presbyterian Church hearkens back to this era. Other significant buildings in the area include the former headquarters of the influential daily newspapers the *Detroit News* and *Detroit Free Press*.

DETROIT CLUB
712 Cass Avenue

The Detroit Club was founded by attorney Samuel T. Douglas and banker Henry Campbell on October 11, 1882, making it the city's oldest private men's social club. When increased membership dictated larger digs, this stately clubhouse was constructed. Designed by Wilson Eyre Jr., the eclectic four-story building with Romanesque and Second Empire influences was completed in 1891 and featured amenities appealing to well-heeled businessmen and politicians of the day, such as a great room, a dining room, small and large meeting rooms, ballrooms, a billiard parlor and guest rooms—all elegantly appointed with custom finishes, furniture and art.

Membership reads like a who's who of local powerbrokers, including movers and shakers in politics, industry, banking and law, such as John Bagley, Hazen S. Pingree, Henry Ford, Walter P. Chrysler and Ransom E. Olds. These men wielded major influence, so it's not surprising that the club would host famous guests such as Presidents Truman, Hoover and Roosevelt; or royalty, as in Prince William of Sweden and the Duke of Windsor; or celebrities such as singer and author Margaret Truman and aviator Charles Lindbergh.

"The Detroit Club was at the epicenter of numerous, pivotal, events effecting Detroit's, and the Nation's, economic growth, consumerism, and industrialism," per club history. A series of meetings held there in 1902 led to the formation of the Automobile Club of Detroit, a national association that still dominates the automobile industry. Between 1944 and 1945, Henry Ford's grandson Henry Ford II regained control of Ford Motor Company from Harry Bennett through mediation sessions held at the club. American automotive icon Lee Iacocca, who spearheaded the development of the Ford Mustang and Pinto, launched his campaign to restore the Statue of Liberty and develop Ellis Island into a museum from the club.

The building, which recently underwent extensive renovations, is now privately owned. Non-members are currently permitted to dine in the restaurant and book overnight stays.

THEODORE LEVIN UNITED STATES COURTHOUSE
231 West Lafayette Boulevard

Named in honor of the late Theodore Levin, a lawyer and United States District Court judge, the ten-story federal courthouse opened in 1934. Polished black stone serves as the base for this limestone-clad, Moderne-style building with Art Deco elements. Relief sculptures of eagles and emblems above the entrance symbolize the building's function as a government agency.

A decorative marble lion fixture found in the "million-dollar courtroom" inside the Theodore Levin Federal Courthouse. *Courtesy of Photographs in Carol M. Highsmith Archive, Library of Congress, Prints and Photographs Division.*

Aside from the many high-profile trials that have taken place here, a unique feature of this building is the chief judge's courtroom on the seventh floor. When the former courthouse, built in 1897, was torn down to make way for the current structure, Chief Judge Arthur Tuttle requested the lavish marble courtroom be disassembled and reassembled in the new building. The opulent courthouse was dubbed the "million-dollar courtroom" by the media at the time because of the expense. Today, the courtroom is priceless.

5. MICHIGAN AVENUE PEOPLE MOVER STATION

Michigan Avenue follows an old Native American path and is one of the first official roads in Michigan. It begins a few blocks east of this station at Campus Martius and travels west across the state. Stagecoaches regularly used the "Old Chicago Road" to travel between Chicago and Detroit.

Some streets in Detroit and the surrounding region are numbered. Michigan Avenue is Zero Mile Road near downtown. Eight Mile Road, the city's northern boundary, is eight miles north of Michigan Avenue. Michigan Avenue eventually angles south, and Ford Road becomes Zero Mile Road just west of Wyoming Street.

Lafayette Greens, a lush urban garden in downtown Detroit, can be found where the historic Lafayette Building once stood. The building was demolished in 2010. *Author's collection.*

WESTIN BOOK CADILLAC
1114 Washington Boulevard

Transforming Washington Boulevard into the "Fifth Avenue of the Midwest" was the goal of the three Book brothers, James Jr., Herbert and Frank, as they undertook several development projects, including a luxury hotel. When the opulent, thirty-three-story Book Cadillac opened in December 1924, it was the tallest hotel in the world. Built at a cost of $14 million, the upscale Italian Renaissance–style hotel designed by Louis Kamper contained over one thousand guest rooms, three dining rooms, three ballrooms, a spacious lobby and a ground-floor retail arcade.

For many years, the "Book" was the top hotel in Detroit for hosting conventions, weddings and high-society events, according to the Westin Book Cadillac website. Prominent guests included presidents, first ladies, civil rights icons, business moguls, movie stars, entertainers, sports figures and more. Even members of the nefarious Purple Gang were reputed guests.

The hotel received a nod from Hollywood in the 1948 Frank Capra movie *State of the Union*, starring Spencer Tracy, Katharine Hepburn and Angela Lansbury. A scene shows industrialist and presidential hopeful Grant Matthews, played by Tracy, in room 2419 preparing for a speech he'll deliver to Detroit's business leaders.

On May 2, 1939, the Detroit Tigers were scheduled to meet the New York Yankees at home. The Yankees' star first baseman, Lou Gehrig, known as the "Iron Horse," met with team manager Joe McCarthy inside the hotel where the team was staying and removed himself from the lineup. Gehrig, who had struggled badly thus far in the season, hadn't missed a game since 1925. This voluntary benching ended Gehrig's record-setting consecutive streak of 2,130 professional baseball games, which wouldn't be broken until Cal Ripken Jr. did so in 1995. The following June, Gehrig was diagnosed with amyotrophic lateral sclerosis (ALS), a progressive neurodegenerative disease that affects nerve cells in the brain and spinal cord. Gehrig would eventually succumb to the disease that prematurely ended his baseball career.

An ornamental relief above the Michigan Avenue entrance pays homage to early influential Detroiters. The figures represent Revolutionary War hero General Anthony Wayne, French founder Antoine De La Mothe Cadillac, Native American chief Pontiac and French nobleman Robert Navarre, whose local civic career spanned French, British and American rule. A statue of Alexander Macomb, Navarre's Detroit-born grandson, stands opposite the hotel's Washington Boulevard entrance. Macomb was

Designed by architect Louis Kamper, the thirty-three-story Book Cadillac was the largest hotel in the world when it opened in December 1924. *Courtesy of Library of Congress.*

the region's largest landowner, and recent historical accounts claim he was also the largest local slave owner.

During the Great Depression, the illustrious hotel faltered but rebounded again under new ownership in the 1940s and flourished over the next two decades. The 1960s ushered in challenging times for the once bustling city and its businesses as the prospering suburbs siphoned people, commerce and economic resources. The hotel struggled financially, something ownership changes and multiple rebranding couldn't overcome. After a nearly sixty-year run, the grand lady closed its doors in 1984 and became another empty landmark in a once thriving downtown.

After sitting vacant for two decades and stripped completely by scrappers, a private developer and the city devised a redevelopment plan. On October 6, 2008, the Westin Book Cadillac reopened its doors following a two-year, $200 million restoration.

BOOK TOWER

1265 Washington Boulevard

This thirty-six-story office tower stands out among the other office buildings downtown because of its unusual design, a fancy Beaux Arts tower and copper roof atop a rather nondescript lower portion and a quirky fire escape, spanning its entire south side.

Book Tower, another Washington Boulevard project of the Book brothers, was briefly the tallest building in the city until the Penobscot Building surpassed it in 1928. The Great Depression halted plans to build an eighty-one-story tower at the opposite end of the adjacent thirteen-story Book Building.

Designed by architect Louis Kamper, Book Tower served as a prestigious address on Washington Boulevard from its opening through the mid-1970s. Its good fortune ended in 1988, when the owners defaulted on the mortgage. After sitting vacant for nearly a decade, the building was purchased by a prominent local developer and is undergoing extensive renovations.

On a humorous note, reliefs of the twelve apostles can be found on the façade of St. Alloysius Catholic Church, located across the street on the east side of Washington Boulevard. Locals like to joke the apostles are gazing longingly at the many nude caryatids (feminine sculptural architectural supports) adorning the Book buildings.

CAPITOL PARK

Griswold Street between State Street and Grand River Avenue

Detroit was Michigan's first capital dating back to the establishment of the Michigan Territory by Congress in 1805 until it was officially moved to Lansing on March 17, 1847, ten years after Michigan achieved statehood.

A red brick Greek Revival building designed by Obed Wait and completed in 1828 served as the territorial courthouse and, later, the courthouse/capitol. Once the capital was moved from Detroit to its permanent location, the building became a public school and library until it burned in 1893. Known as Union School, it was once Detroit's only high school.

A statue in the park pays tribute to Michigan's first governor, Stevens T. Mason. The "boy governor" was only twenty-four years old when first elected to this position in October 1835 after voters ratified a state constitution. His official governorship was delayed by nearly two years

A Detroit Publishing Company photo taken between 1911 and 1920 shows the Garrick Theater and Dime Building from a Capitol Park vantage point, looking south on Griswold Street. *Courtesy of Library of Congress.*

until a dispute between Michigan and Ohio known as the Toledo War was settled. When Michigan was admitted to the Union on January 26, 1837, he was reelected governor.

Mason advocated for a statewide education system and secured land in Ann Arbor for the future site of the University of Michigan. The Panic of 1837 rocked Michigan's economy, and Mason took the heat. Rather than addressing his critics, Mason chose not to seek reelection. After completing his term as governor, Mason abruptly moved to New York City, where he practiced law until his untimely death on January 4, 1843, at the young age of thirty-one. Originally buried in New York Marble Cemetery, his remains were later exhumed and reburied in the base of the statue at Capitol Park. The statue has been moved within the park three times. Some say Mason's spirit haunts the park, because his remains have been disturbed so many times.

The David Stott building is one of several notable buildings surrounding the park. Built for the heirs of the flour king David Stott, the thirty-eight-story skyscraper designed by Donaldson and Meier opened in June 1929. It was the final Art Deco building constructed in Detroit prior to the nation's economic collapse. A few distinct features include the custom reddish-brown brick and colorful tile spandrels by George R. Mehling. The speed of the elevators—eight hundred feet per minute—was a big deal at the time of construction.

The twelve-story Spier and Rohns–designed Chamber of Commerce Building at 1212 Griswold was completed in 1895. It's Detroit's oldest existing skyscraper. The Finney Barn, a safe house on the Underground Railroad, occupied this spot in the 1850s.

6. TIMES SQUARE PEOPLE MOVER STATION

This station is named for the *Detroit Times*, a newspaper published locally from 1842 until 1960. Its offices stood where the Rosa Parks Transit Station is located.

MICHIGAN BUILDING
220 Bagley Avenue

A historic marker outside the former Michigan Theatre denotes an early residence of Henry and Clara Ford. It was here in 1896 that Ford built his first car, a quadricycle, in the storage shed behind their rented duplex. The shed would be re-created in 1933 at Greenfield Village using reclaimed bricks from a wall near the Bagley Avenue residence.

In the 1920s, this once residential area was prime for redevelopment. The Michigan Building, a thirteen-story office tower and adjoining four-thousand-seat palatial movie theater, went up. Once the talk of Detroit, this opulent theater would later meet the fate of other movie theaters and officially closed in the early 1970s. Plans to tear down the theater to make a parking lot to service a large office tenant had to be altered when it was determined the demolition would damage the structural integrity of the adjoining office building. A 160-car parking garage was built within the footprint of the old theater. Remnants of the theater's grandeur can be seen inside the parking garage, making for a unique tourist attraction. To add to the lore, many movies have been filmed inside the parking structure, including scenes from *Eight Mile* starring Marshall Mathers, also known as Eminem.

Local author and historian Dan Austin eloquently summarized the theater's tragic fate on his HistoricDetroit.org blog: "In a twist that is as sad as it is ironic, the theater was built on the site of the small garage where Henry Ford built his first automobile, the quadricycle. The site of the automobile's birthplace replaced by a movie theater, reclaimed by the automobile."

To the right of the Michigan Building is another example of a once grand theater. The former United Artists Theater, which has been vacant for decades, is owned by a major developer that owns multiple nearby properties. No renovation plans have been released. To the left across Cass Avenue is the Leland Hotel. The once posh hotel named after Henry M. Leland, founder of luxury automotive brands Lincoln and Cadillac, has been converted into apartments, and its current state is a far cry from its former grandeur.

GAR BUILDING
1942 West Grand River Boulevard

This quirky turreted castle, which seems more appropriate standing guard on the Rhine River than on a triangular patch in downtown Detroit, has long piqued the interest of locals and visitors. Designed by Julian Hess and Richard Raseman, it served as a fellowship hall for veterans of the Civil War who were members of the fraternal organization Grand Army of the Republic (GAR). Tip: Correct pronunciation is G-A-R, not gar.

After the war, men joined various groups to reestablish ties with those with whom they had forged bonds on the battlefield. The Grand Army of the Republic, founded in 1866, emerged as the most powerful of these groups. While men initially met to reminisce about their shared experiences, the conversations quickly turned to serious issues such as jobs, healthcare and monetary compensation. According to the Sons of Union Veterans of the Civil War national website, members joined "first for camaraderie and then for political power." With membership surpassing 400,000 by 1890, the GAR wielded significant political clout.

Being the state's largest city and a major contributor to its war effort, it was only fitting that Detroit should have a memorial hall that reflected its stature. Many of the city's influential businessmen and politicians had served in the war.

Completed in 1890, the GAR Building is one of a few remaining nineteenth-century commercial buildings. The building originally included thirteen retail shops and a bank on the first floor and a small auditorium on the fourth floor.

By the 1930s, GAR membership had aged and died off, so the building was no longer needed to serve its original purpose. Ownership reverted to the City of Detroit, which had supplied part of the initial construction funds. Vacancy plagued the building throughout the twentieth century, and it was last used as a recreation center in the 1980s before being boarded up again. On February 13, 1986, the building was added to the National Register of Historic Places.

In November 2011, the owners of Mindfield, a local media production company, purchased the building and began extensive restoration and renovations. Upon completion, they relocated their corporate headquarters here, and two popular restaurants are now open on the main floor.

7. GRAND CIRCUS PARK PEOPLE MOVER STATION

This People Mover station adjoins the David Whitney Building, named for the lumber, real estate and shipping magnate, once one of Detroit's wealthiest residents. Designed by Daniel Burnham and Company, it opened in 1915 with retail stores on the first floor and medical offices on the upper floors. Many Detroiters have fond, or not so fond, memories of trips to the building for doctor and dentist appointments. The building reopened in 2014 as the Aloft Hotel after undergoing extensive restoration and renovation.

The David Whitney Building central light court provides an airy, bright ambiance, giving this 1915 Neoclassical beauty a timeless appeal. *Rod Arroyo.*

GRAND CIRCUS PARK
Woodward Avenue between Park and Adams Avenues

The thirty-one-acre park bisected by Woodward Avenue was built in 1836 and is a vestige of Judge Woodward's plan for Detroit implemented after the fire of 1805 (see Campus Martius). The half-circle or crescent-shaped park features fountains dedicated to inventor Thomas Alva Edison and Michigan's twentieth governor, Russell Alger.

Made of limestone, the Edison Memorial Fountain was installed in 1929 to commemorate Light's Golden Jubilee celebrating the fiftieth anniversary of Edison's invention of the electric lamp. The Beaux-Arts bronze Russell Alger Memorial Fountain is another collaboration by sculptor Daniel French and architect Henry Bacon. Bacon designed the famous Lincoln Memorial in Washington, D.C., with French designing the epic statue of Abraham

The statue of beloved Detroit mayor and "idol of the people" Hazen Pingree at Grand Circus Park. *Courtesy of Library of Congress.*

Lincoln sitting inside. Dedicated in 1921, the Alger Memorial was cast by Gorham Manufacturing Company and depicts a female personification of Michigan. Civil War veterans commissioned the work.

Statues of two former Detroit mayors, Hazen S. Pingree and William Cotter Maybury, flank the north ends of the park. Pingree served as mayor from 1890 to 1897. His progressive measures during tough economic times and advocacy for the "little guy" earned him the moniker of "idol of the people." Maybury, who was Pingree's arch enemy and rival, followed Pingree's term as mayor.

MERCHANT'S ROW

Woodward Avenue between Park and Michigan Avenues

Designated a historic district to commemorate the once thriving shopping district spanning several blocks on Woodward Avenue and adjacent streets, this area was home to prominent retailers such as the J.L. Hudson Company, Detroit's beloved department store (see Cadillac Centre entry); S.S. Kresge, one of the nation's foremost twentieth-century discount stores, renamed

Kmart in 1977; Grinnell Brothers Music Store, once the world's largest distributor of pianos; Sanders, our favorite confectionary and soda fountain; Himmelhoch's; Winkelman's; Three Sisters; Crowley's; and others. Retail is slowly returning to the district with the opening of several major national and international chains and a few independent stores. The luxury brand Shinola will open a boutique hotel in the district soon as well.

CENTRAL UNITED METHODIST CHURCH
23 East Adams Avenue

Central United's roots date back to 1804, when Reverend Daniel Freeman, a circuit-riding preacher, delivered the first Methodist sermon in Michigan at Council House in Detroit. The church is known as the "conscience of Detroit" because of its steadfast involvement in social issues. The congregation was instrumental in getting capital punishment abolished in Michigan in 1846. "Central is intentionally and proudly a multi-racial, multi-everything church, believing that our diversity is 'God's work of art.'" Dr. Martin Luther King Jr. spoke from the pulpit on several occasions.

The cornerstone of this Gordon W. Lloyd–designed church was laid on July 3, 1867. While many early members argued the location was too far from downtown, trustees have fielded numerous offers over the years from business leaders willing to pay almost any price for the property. The proposals have been declined, as they believe downtown Detroit needs Central United Methodist Church and its influence far more than it needs one more place of business.

A vintage postcard of Grand Circus Park looking north on Woodward Avenue shows the Thomas Edison Fountain on the left and Central United Methodist Church, known as the conscience of Detroit, on the right. *Author's collection.*

Fox Theatre
2211 Woodward Avenue

Built as the flagship of motion picture mogul William Fox's national chain of theaters, this opulent movie palace opened in 1928. Designed by internationally renowned theater architect C. Howard Crane, the unrestrained décor favoring East Asian, Indian and Egyptian influences incorporates rich jewel tones, brass, massive ornamental pillars and fanciful plaster figures in the shapes of monkeys, serpents, stately lions, elephants, butterflies and deities. Twenty artists worked for nine months to create the clay designs later reproduced as ornamental plaster found throughout the theater.

An imposing multistory marquee hangs above the theater's front entrance leading into the enormous six-story lobby, which occupies half a block. Two fabulous organs can be found inside the Fox. A three-manual, thirteen-rank Moller organ sits in the lobby, and a massive manual thirty-six-rank Wurlitzer, one of only five such instruments constructed especially for the largest Fox Theatres in the country, presides over the theater, which seats over five thousand people.

While some may view the theater's sumptuous design as over the top, a contractor quoted in the *Detroit Free Press* days after the Fox's opening said theaters can be overdone, garish or tomblike. "The new Fox has struck the desirable medium and is in excellent architectural taste."

The illuminated historic Fox Theatre marquee hints at the grandeur found inside this flagship Art Deco movie palace. *Rod Arroyo.*

According to a National Public Radio (NPR) article, "The exotic and elaborate decor helped people from all social classes in Detroit escape from the monotony of their everyday lives."

The innovative Fox Theatre ushered in a new era. It was the world's first movie theater built with a patented, in-house, sound-on-film system called Movietone, which allowed for the showing of talking pictures. Other theaters had to be retrofitted with the proper equipment to show movies with sound. Detroit's largest theater was second in size only to New

York's once illustrious Roxy Theatre, which opened the previous year and tragically met the wrecking ball in 1960.

Opening night on September 21, 1928, was quite the extravaganza. The Fox grand orchestra performed overtures and waltzes. The *Evolution of Transportation*, an eight-part pageant featuring actors, ballet dancers and a chorus, paid homage to Detroit's history of innovation. A George Bernard Shaw screen debut, a colorful short highlighting old Naples and the feature film *Screen Angel* fully immersed the audience in the theater's proprietary screen and sound technology.

In addition to movies, the theater offered live productions and performances. Celebrities such as Shirley Temple and Elvis Presley made appearances, as did Motown greats. For many years beginning in the 1960s, the annual Motown Revue hosted between Christmas and New Year's Day was a much-anticipated holiday event.

Although the theater never closed, attendance suffered in the 1970s and '80s, as did the quality of movies shown. In 1987, the theater was purchased by pizza magnates Mike and Marion Ilitch, owners of Olympia Entertainment, and restored to its former glory the following year at a cost of $12 million.

The Fox lives on today as a premier entertainment venue featuring a variety of live productions. If possible, catch a show and revel in the theater's magnificence.

Comerica Park
2100 Woodward Avenue

Home of Major League Baseball team the Detroit Tigers since April 2000, this outdoor ballpark is a popular destination for sports enthusiasts as well as visitors seeking fun photo opportunities. Large and small groups assembling outside the main gate and posing with the fifteen-foot-tall tiger are a familiar sight. This heroic-sized landmark designed by New York artist Michael Keropian is one of nine fiberglass tigers weighing two to four thousand pounds displayed at the park. "Decade Monuments" positioned throughout the main concourse of the forty-thousand-plus-seat stadium pay homage to the team's twentieth-century history with artifacts pertinent to each era.

East of the ballpark lies Ford Field, home to the Detroit Lions, the city's professional football team. The stadium, whose maximum capacity is sixty-five thousand, opened in 2002 and incorporated the warehouse of beloved department store J.L. Hudson's into its construction. A historic marker

A vintage postcard of the YMCA razed along with many buildings to make way for Comerica Park. *Author's collection.*

near the St. Antoine gate pays tribute to Paradise Valley, once Detroit's African American business and entertainment district: "From the 1930s into the 1950s Paradise Valley bustled around the clock. Nightspots like 606 Horseshoe Lounge, Club Plantation, and Club 666 featured entertainers such as Duke Ellington, Dinah Washington, the Ink Spots, and Sarah Vaughan. Blacks who performed elsewhere in Michigan were excluded from white hotels and stayed in the valley. Beginning in the 1940s, urban renewal projects, the construction of freeways, and new development devastated African American neighborhoods, including Paradise Valley. The Valley's last three structures, located along St. Antoine Street, were demolished in 2000."

Many prominent buildings were demolished in the late 1990s to make way for the twin stadiums, including those housing the Detroit College of Law, Young Men's Christian Association and Young Women's Christian Association. The Gem/Century Building and Elwood Bar managed to escape the wrecking ball because local real estate investor and preservationist Chuck Forbes decided to relocate them.

According to the Detroit Historical Society's *Encyclopedia of Detroit*, Forbes wanted to preserve for future generations an example of a small, medium and large theater from the 1920s. He purchased the State (now Fillmore Detroit), Fox and Gem Theatres in the late 1970s and early '80s and is often credited with initiating the revival of Detroit's faded movie palaces. Although Forbes sold the Fox Theatre (see Fox Theatre entry), he restored the others. After completing painstaking renovations, Forbes couldn't bear to see the Gem/Century razed as part of the stadium development, so in 1997, he agreed to move it 1,850 feet or five blocks to 333 Madison Street. The move garnered a spot for the building (weighing approximately five million pounds) in the *Guinness Book of World Records* as the heaviest building moved on rubber wheels.

The circa 1936 Art Moderne–style Elwood Bar, designed by Charles Noble, moved to 300 East Adams Street, between Comerica Park and Ford Field.

73

8. BROADWAY PEOPLE MOVER STATION

The two-block historic district attached to this stop was developed in the late 1800s as a commercial area catering to women's trades and included businesses such as hairdressers, florists, corset makers and fashionable clothiers.

DETROIT OPERA HOUSE
1526 Broadway

Now home to the Michigan Opera Theatre, the opera house opened in 1922 as the Capitol Theatre, one of many performance venues surrounding Grand Circus Park. Designed by C. Howard Crane, this opulent theater seated 3,500 and was the fifth largest in the world. The theater underwent several name changes over the years and closed down in the '70s and again in the '80s. The Michigan Opera Theatre purchased the building in 1988. Architect Eric J. Hill oversaw the major restoration. Luciano Pavarotti performed at the 1996 grand opening gala.

DETROIT ATHLETIC CLUB (DAC)
241 Madison Street

The original male social club was organized in 1887 as a gathering spot for members to watch or participate in sporting events. Inadequate social facilities and sources to generate revenue caused membership to decline, but when private social clubs gained popularity around the country, members experienced renewed interest in reviving their club. It's been reported that Packard Motor Car Company president Henry B. Joy, a founding DAC member and its third president, favored resurrecting the club "to get the men of the automobile industry out of the saloons on Woodward Avenue."

Celebrated local architect Albert Kahn drew upon his travels to Rome and Florence when designing this ornate six-story Renaissance-inspired structure whose large fourth-floor windows resemble those found at the Palazzo Farnese in Rome. Interior plans called for three distinct sections dedicated to social functions, athletics and overnight residential suites with amenities catering to the well-heeled, such as handball courts, a swimming pool, a billiard room and Turkish baths. Although updated over the years, the building remains true to Kahn's original vision when it was completed in 1915.

WURLITZER BUILDING
1509 Broadway

Vacant for decades, this fourteen-story Robert Finn–designed building was one of the retail outlets of Wurlitzer Company, which billed itself as the "world's largest music house." After the music store closed, the building was occupied by other tenants before closing in 1982. The Wurlitzer and neighboring Metropolitan Building stood in ruin for decades. After undergoing extensive restoration, the Wurlitzer reopened in early 2018 as the Siren Hotel. The Metropolitan will reopen soon as a hotel too.

Wurlitzer Building in the foreground, once one of the largest music stores in the world, reopened recently as a boutique hotel after sitting vacant for decades. *Rod Arroyo.*

9. CADILLAC CENTER PEOPLE MOVER STATION

Pewabic tiles donated by the owners of the now-defunct Stroh's Brewery make up the beautiful arched installation at this station, which provides convenient access to businesses located north of Gratiot.

ROSE AND ROBERT SKILLMAN BRANCH
OF THE DETROIT PUBLIC LIBRARY
121 Gratiot Avenue

Designed by the architectural firm of Smith, Hinchman & Grylls, the Skillman Library opened in 1932. The library houses the National Automotive History Collection (NAHC), regarded as the nation's premier

Detroit People Mover track in front of Skillman Library. Note the flag flying over the David Whitney Building, now the Aloft Hotel. Broderick Tower is in the distance. *Rod Arroyo.*

public automotive archive documenting the history and development of the automobile and other forms of motorized, wheeled land transportation in the United States and abroad.

THE BELT
Between Grand River and Gratiot Avenue

A former unsightly alley has been transformed into a popular outdoor art gallery in the city's former garment district, hence the name The Belt. The public space highlights murals and installations by local, national and international artists. Even the surrounding ten-story Z Garage features funky, bold murals on each level of the parking structure.

"The Belt," an alley in Detroit's old garment district, has been transformed into an outdoor art gallery and popular gathering place. *Courtesy of Bedrock.*

J.L. HUDSON BUILDING
1206 Woodward Avenue

This vacant lot is where the flagship store of Detroit's most beloved retail department chain once stood. Named after company founder Joseph Lowthian Hudson, J.L. Hudson's first store opened in the late nineteenth century adjacent to the former opera house located a block south of here. Construction began on this structure in 1911, and it underwent several additions before completion in 1946.

Shoppers enjoyed thirty-three levels of merchandise spread throughout five basements, a mezzanine and multiple stories. At one time, Hudson's was the tallest department store in the world and second in square footage only

A view of the once thriving shopping district. J.L. Hudson department store was located on vacant space on the left. Book Tower is the tall building in the distance. *Rod Arroyo.*

to Macy's in New York. To the dismay of locals, Hudson's was sold off to Marshall Field's and then Macy's. The main store closed in 1986 and was imploded in 1998. Ground was broken in late 2017 for construction of a modern, mixed-use project that includes a residential tower taller than the Marriott Hotel at the Renaissance Center.

10. GREEKTOWN PEOPLE MOVER STATION

Greektown is a popular entertainment area with many restaurants, bars and a casino. While Greek immigrants set up shop here in the mid-1900s, the area was originally settled by Germans and later African Americans who migrated from the South. While there are still a handful of Greek restaurants, you'll now find a mix ranging from American burger fare to Irish or Cajun.

Circa 1980s photo shows a bevy of Greek-owned businesses once dominating the popular Greektown entertainment district. J.L. Hudson's, once the world's tallest department store, was imploded in 1998. *Rod Arroyo.*

SECOND BAPTIST CHURCH
441 Monroe Avenue

Initially a small wooden structure built for German worshipers, it was purchased by thirteen self-emancipated slaves who founded Second Baptist Church. The mother church of all Detroit African American churches, Second Baptist is also the oldest African American church in Michigan and possibly the Midwest.

The church served as the Croghan Street station on the Underground Railroad, and church historians claim Pastor Robert L. Bradbury loaned Henry Ford $500 to get his automotive company off the ground. Henry Ford never forgot this act and employed any African Americans who presented a letter from the church. Nobel Peace Prize recipient Ralph Bunche was baptized here. Notable guest speakers at the church include Frederick Douglass and Dr. Martin Luther King Jr.

TRAPPERS ALLEY

The block where Greektown Casino stands was once a large-scale fur tannery established in 1889. When demand declined in the 1920s, the tannery closed, and the space was occupied by many different tenants. In the 1980s, the space opened as a unique marketplace called Trappers Alley with many of the industrial and architectural elements retained. Trappers Alley was incorporated into the design of the casino, which opened in 2000.

Greektown, a popular entertainment district today, was initially settled by Germans and then became a bustling commercial and residential area for Detroit's early black residents. *Courtesy of Bedrock.*

OLD ST. MARY'S
646 Monroe Street

Built for German immigrants in 1885, this beautiful church designed by Peter Dederichs is known for its soaring ceilings and many grottoes. It's the third oldest Roman Catholic church in Detroit. The parish thrives today with mass held daily to accommodate downtown workers. It's a popular venue for weddings.

FRANK MURPHY HALL OF JUSTICE
1441 St. Antoine Street

Built in 1968, the courthouse is named for Supreme Court justice Frank Murphy, who was appointed to this position in 1940 by President Franklin D. Roosevelt and served until his death at age fifty-nine on July 19, 1949. Known for his liberal views, Murphy wrote a scathing rebuke in response to the 1944 majority ruling in *Korematsu v. United States*, which upheld the constitutionality of the government's internment of Japanese Americans during World War II. He described the decision as the "legalization of racism."

In his earlier career as a Detroit Circuit Court judge, Murphy presided over an important 1925 civil rights trial in which Dr. Ossian Sweet and members of his family stood trial for murder. Sweet, an African American, moved his family into a white neighborhood. An angry mob of white residents retaliated by congregating outside the home and lobbing rocks and threats at the family huddling in fear inside. Shots fired from inside the house killed one of the intimidators. High-profile defense attorney Clarence Darrow represented the Sweets, and in a stunning verdict, the all-white jury acquitted the defendants of murder.

Hand of God sculpture by Carl Milles stands in front of the Frank Murphy Hall of Justice. Both are tributes to the politician and jurist who influenced local and national legislation. *Author's collection.*

Murphy had an impressive political career, including stints as mayor of Detroit during the early years of the Great Depression and thirty-fifth governor of Michigan. During Murphy's mayoral tenure, he lobbied for federal aid to cities, implemented programs to feed the hungry and balanced city books. As governor, he's credited with helping to resolve the 1937 strike by General Motors workers.

He is ranked seventh-best mayor in the book *The American Mayor: The Best & Worst Big-City Leaders* and just three spots below Hazen Pingree, another beloved Detroit mayor. Author Melvin E. Holli wrote:

> *Murphy deserves wider recognition, especially because his postmayoral career of upward movement is remarkable and striking for a mayor. After service in city hall, Murphy rose rapidly to become governor-general of the Philippines, then governor of Michigan, and next a U.S. Attorney General. He ended his public career as a U.S. Supreme Court justice. Few big-city mayors have experienced such dramatic and visible upward political mobility. Even for the best of them, the mayor's chair is generally a terminal office.*

Outside the courthouse stands *The Hand of God*, one of the final works by Carl Milles, a noted sculptor and former professor at Cranbrook Academy of Art in Bloomfield Hills, Michigan. Controversy erupted at the statue's 1949 unveiling because the newly created man whom God holds in his hand is naked. The "inappropriate" commission was placed in storage until UAW leader Walter Reuther, who had been privy to the design, disregarded objections and had the statue installed on a tall pedestal.

Recently, an agreement was reached between Wayne County executive Warren Evans and a prominent developer to relocate the criminal justice campus—including the courthouse, a juvenile detention center, two jails and an unfinished jail—to another location and redevelop this prime downtown real estate. No word yet if the new courthouse will bear Murphy's name.

11. BRICKTOWN PEOPLE MOVER STATION

Bricktown derives its name from the red brick row houses and commercial buildings once commonly found here. Only a few of the original structures remain. Two important historic markers denote the former site of the William Webb house, where abolitionists John Brown and

Frederick Douglass met while in Detroit, and the home of Underground Railroad conductor George DeBaptiste. While there is no historic marker acknowledging it, Senator Jacob Merritt Howard's house once stood at Larned and Hastings Streets (now I-375). A founding member of the Republican Party, Senator Merritt co-authored the Thirteenth, Fourteenth and Fifteenth Amendments to the Constitution, which abolished slavery, provided for citizenship and provided the right to vote, respectively.

ALEXANDER CHAPOTON HOUSE
511 Beaubian Street

Alexander Chapoton, a descendant of one of Detroit's original French families, built this Queen Anne–style home in 1885 on what was then the Beaubien farm, which extended all the way to the Detroit River. It's one of the few remaining brick structures from this period. Many were demolished and replaced with parking lots.

A prominent nineteenth-century contractor, Chapoton built many of the earlier notable downtown buildings, including the Detroit Opera House, Russell House and Michigan Exchange Hotel. While these buildings no longer exist, another nearby example of his work does. The six-story Romanesque Revival Globe Tobacco Building, located at 407 East Fort Street, is the oldest tobacco manufactory extant in Detroit.

Artist Anna Muccioli painted the Asian-inspired mural on the building's exterior south-side wall in 1981, shortly after she and her husband, Joseph, purchased and restored the building to house her art gallery. The couple, now deceased, lobbied to get the Chapoton House designated as a historic building.

ST. ANDREW'S HALL
431 East Congress Street

This structure was built for the St. Andrew's Scottish Society of Detroit in 1907. It remained a popular social club for "Scotchmen and descendants" until World War II, when membership dropped. The society adapted by renting out the facility so other organizations could host meetings and events. In the 1980s, St. Andrew's evolved into a popular, intimate music venue that hosted legendary established artists such as Iggy Pop, Bob Dylan, Paul Simon and groundbreaking '90s bands such as Nirvana, R.E.M., Red

Hot Chili Peppers, Pearl Jam and Soundgarden. The music continues into the current millennium with contemporary acts such as John Mayer, Adele, Eminem and others, according to venue operator Live Nation.

12. OUTSIDE CENTRAL BUSINESS DISTRICT

CHRIST CHURCH
960 East Jefferson Avenue

Built in 1863, Christ Church is considered the oldest Protestant church in Detroit still in its original location. Designed by architect Gordon W. Lloyd in the American Gothic style, it's constructed of limestone and sandstone and features a squared-off Germanic roof. The church possesses several irreplaceable stained-glass windows done by Tiffany, Franz Mayer and Company and J. Wippell and Company. The former church on this site was designed by Montgomery Miegs, a member of the congregation. Miegs also designed Arlington Cemetery.

SIBLEY HOUSE
976 East Jefferson Avenue

Now used as the rectory for neighboring Christ Church, this single-family home was built for the family of Mayor Solomon Sibley in 1848. It is one of the oldest intact commercial or residential buildings in Detroit. The Charles Trowbridge House, located a few blocks east at 1380 East Jefferson Avenue, was built in 1826 and is considered the oldest structure in Detroit.

Built in 1848 for Judge Solomon Sibley, Detroit's first mayor, Sibley House is one of the oldest homes in the city still standing. *Courtesy of Library of Congress.*

MIDTOWN • SITES OF INTEREST

1. **Fisher Theater**
2. **Cadillac Place**
3. **Ford Piquette Plant**
4. **Ferry Street Historic District**
5. **Detroit Historical Museum**
6. **Park Shelton**
7. **Detroit Public Library (Main)**
8. **Detroit Institute of Arts**
9. **Scarab Club**
10. **Charles Wright Museum of African American History**
11. **Maccabees Building**
12. **Wayne State University Campus**
13. **Cathedral Church of St. Paul**
14. **Historic First Congregational Church**
15. **The Whitney**
16. **Canfield Historic District**
17. **Orchestra Hall**

CHAPTER 3

MIDTOWN

A cultural Mecca, Midtown is home to historic landmarks, prestigious educational and medical institutions, five major museums, world-class theaters, music venues, beautiful churches, funky galleries, community gardens, popular restaurants and bars and unique retail shops. The influence of the City Beautiful movement, which swept the nation following the 1893 World's Columbian Exposition held in Chicago, can be found in the white limestone or marble façades of many of the buildings located in this area.

Explore this area on foot or via QLine, Detroit's new streetcar system, which travels north and south on Woodward Avenue with numerous stations situated throughout downtown and midtown. Regular fare is $1.50 for three hours or $3.00 for a day pass.

1. FISHER THEATRE/BUILDING

3011 West Grand Boulevard

Often referred to as Detroit's largest art object, this lovely Art Deco masterpiece was constructed for the seven Fisher brothers—Frederick, Charles, William, Lawrence, Edward, Alfred and Howard—founders of Fisher Body Company, established in 1908. Originally from Ohio, the

Inside the Fisher Building, Detroit's "largest art object." View from the third-floor balcony overlooking the opulent lobby. *Rod Arroyo.*

brothers adapted their nineteenth-century horse-drawn carriage-making skills to the new era of horseless carriages. They perfected the concept of the enclosed auto body, which made year-round driving possible. General Motors eventually purchased the company from the brothers but dissolved this division, a major local employer, in 1984. Many people still remember the iconic Body by Fisher logo and emblem. A beautiful rendition can be found inside the building affixed above the opulent theater doors.

This Albert Kahn–designed twenty-eight-story marvel opened in 1928. The interior and exterior of this "cathedral to commerce" were built almost entirely out of granite and marble. The base of the building exterior extending fifty feet up is finished in polished Minnesota pink marble and Oriental granite.

Construction costs were $9 million, with one-quarter spent on decorative elements such as gold leaf, brass, murals and mosaics. The exquisite light fixtures, each one slightly different, lining the arcade epitomize the Art Deco era. Hungarian artist Geza Maroti designed the arcade's striking painted ceiling treatment, and the New York firms of Ricci and Zari and Anthony DiLorenzo created most of the plasterwork, stonework and ornamental bronze. Corrado Parducci, credited with making Detroit beautiful, apprenticed under Ricci and worked for DiLorenzo before permanently relocating to Detroit.

The building's original 3,500-seat theater was completed in a Mayan temple theme, which radiated with gold and ivory ornamentation. Tropical plants including banana trees filled the lobby, as did a pond stocked with goldfish and turtles. The five talking macaws were a favorite attraction of theatergoers. In 1961, the theater underwent a $3 million renovation after being purchased by the Nederlander Organization. Done in a mid-century aesthetic, the theater now seats almost 3,000 and is the place to catch Broadway productions.

Circa 1940s photo of the main corridor in the Fisher Building. The Art Deco light fixtures still amaze visitors. *Courtesy of Library of Congress.*

The Fisher brothers wanted this building, located a distance from downtown, to be a one-stop destination where affluent clientele could park their cars in the covered garage and shop, dine, catch a show or visit professionals such as doctors, lawyers and accountants while never leaving the building.

This landmark is known for its illuminated gold tower, which can be seen miles away. Originally, the hipped roof was clad with tiles faced in gold leaf, which were paved over with asphalt during World War II as a precaution against enemy attacks. Unfortunately, the asphalt couldn't be removed.

As stunning as this building is, it's only a fraction of the original construction plan, which featured a massive sixty-story tower in between this and another twenty-eight-story tower. The Depression hit, and those plans were nixed.

2. CADILLAC PLACE

3044 West Grand Boulevard

Designed by Albert Kahn, this landmark office building served as the headquarters for General Motors from 1923 to 2001, when the automotive manufacturer moved operations to the Renaissance Center. After much persuasion, President William C. Durant agreed to its construction, and groundbreaking on the fifteen-story, Neoclassic-style building occurred on June 2, 1919. Initial plans called for the new headquarters building to be named after Durant, but when the president was ousted due to corporate politics, it was renamed General Motors Building.

Faced in limestone, the building consists of four fifteen-story structures rising from a two-story base, a design feature that provided the hundreds of individual offices ample access to natural light. The interior features beautiful decorative elements of the era befitting the stature of the auto maker. Many of the surrounding buildings constructed later were affiliated with GM.

Renovated between 2000 and 2002 and renamed Cadillac Place, today the building is occupied by State of Michigan government offices.

Cadillac Place, a landmark Albert Kahn–designed office building, houses government offices for the State of Michigan. From 1923 to 2001, it served as the headquarters for General Motors. *Courtesy of Library of Congress.*

3. FORD PIQUETTE AVENUE PLANT

461 Piquette Avenue

The birthplace of the Model T may be one of the most important automotive heritage sites in the world. Here, inside the experimental room often referred to as the "secret room" located on the third floor of this former automobile factory, a talented team assembled behind closed doors to develop this legendary vehicle. After months of testing and redesigning, the first Model T available for sale debuted on September 27, 1908.

The Model T, dubbed the Tin Lizzy, was truly revolutionary. Prior to its launch, cars were expensive, and only the wealthy could afford them. To compensate for horrendous roads, which were really dirt paths filled with ruts and bumps, early cars were heavy, rigid and cumbersome to drive. The

The birthplace of the Model T, the Ford Piquette Plant is the first factory built specifically for Ford Motor Company. *Rod Arroyo.*

Model T addressed these major issues that limited car ownership. Ford's use of French-made steel vanadium alloy (V-steel) in the Model T's chassis resulted in a highly durable car at half the overall weight of the competition. "The car was everything Henry Ford had hoped and more: light weight, inexpensive, easy to drive and repair, performed well on bad roads, and seated five," states the museum's official website.

Pre-production publicity garnered a flood of orders from America's farmers, rural families and others who appreciated an "efficient, rugged, low-priced auto." While only eleven Model Ts were manufactured in the first month following its release, the Piquette Avenue plant would see production of twelve thousand cars over the next fifteen months. To keep up with demand for the popular car, a new Ford plant was built in Highland Park in 1909, with automobile production officially transferred to the new facility in January 1910. Henry Ford would witness the fifteen millionth Model T roll off the Highland Park assembly line on May 27, 1927.

The Model T made automobile ownership accessible and affordable to the masses and provided them with a mode of transportation that encompassed easy mobility, self-reliance and a sense of freedom never seen before. It set the stage for an era of growth that saw a network of roads and freeways built across the country, high-paying jobs in manufacturing and ancillary industries and unlimited opportunities for ordinary people with innovative ideas to become extremely wealthy and the wealthy elite even richer.

In December 1999, ninety-one years after its introduction, the Model T's impact on the world was recognized when it garnered first place in the Car of the Century competition. The highly regarded contest's lengthy elimination process relied on respected international industry experts, automotive journalists and the general public to determine the most influential automobile of the twentieth century.

Built in 1904, the Victorian-style, three-story brick building designed by Detroit architects Field, Hinchman and Smith was modeled after New England textile mills. Built during the early stages of industrial electric lighting and before air conditioning, the factory design relied on 355 windows to provide light and ventilation. Fire safety features included dividing the long, narrow building into four sections that could be closed off by three heavy-duty fire doors that are still in place today. Each section had its own fire escape, and a twenty-five-thousand-gallon water tank on the roof fed an automatic sprinkler system.

This was the second home of Ford Motor Company, which had only been formed the previous year, on June 16, 1903, by Henry Ford and a group of investors. While twelve investors contributed cash, Henry provided expertise, passion and hard work. The partnership worked, and a year later, Ford Motor Company was building its first state-of-the-art brick factory. A few years later, Henry, who was vice president when the company formed, would buy out his partners and become president of Ford Motor Company.

The Ford Piquette Avenue Plant was built in an area called Milwaukee Junction, a nickname formed from two nearby intersecting railroad lines: Detroit & Milwaukee and Chicago, Detroit & Canada Grand Trunk Junction. The railroad had long helped local industries distribute their products to national markets, so it made sense for automotive manufacturers and suppliers to locate here as well. Anderson Electric Car Company, Brush Motor Car Company, Cadillac Automobile Company, Hupp Motor Car, Packard Motor Car Company, Regal Motor Car Company and E-M-F Company all had factories here. When Ford moved production to its Highland Park factory, the Studebaker Corporation purchased the building and used it to load automobiles onto railroad cars. Per a museum docent, it was easier to do it this way than risk blocking Woodward Avenue and incurring a fine of one hundred silver dollars. Because of the rich automotive history within these few blocks, Milwaukee Junction is called the "cradle of automotive history."

Ford Piquette Avenue Plant visitors step inside the oldest automotive plant in the world open to the public. They're able to visit the "experimental room" where the Model T was conceived, view Henry Ford's personal office re-created from original photographs to look like it did when the automaker occupied it, learn about the stationary assembly process used to mass produce cars before Ford introduced the moving assembly line and see several original Model Ts, including a few red ones. For a car commonly known for its availability in black only, visitors discover that wasn't always the case.

In this humble building listed in the National Register of Historic Places, the car that put the world on wheels was born. Two other legends began here too: Henry Ford, who up to this time had experienced two failed efforts at launching car companies, and Ford Motor Company, now a global powerhouse still known for its innovation. Pretty heady history, don't you agree? That's why visiting the historic Ford Piquette Avenue Plant is a definite Detroit must-do.

For hours of operation and admission fees, call or check out their website: fordpiquetteplant.org.

4. EAST FERRY STREET HISTORIC DISTRICT

Corner of Woodward Avenue and Ferry Street

Step back in time to one of the toniest turn-of-the-twentieth-century neighborhoods and home to industrialists, furriers, real estate speculators and silver mine owners. The neighborhood is noteworthy as it later became a desired address for wealthy and influential African Americans. Ferry Street (formerly avenue) derives its name from the prosperous nineteenth-century landowner and seed merchant Dexter M. Ferry, president of D.M. Ferry Seed Company, whose commercial gardens once occupied fields a few blocks farther east.

The enchanting castle built for the Colonel Frank J. Hecker family fronting Woodward Avenue at Ferry Street epitomizes the opulent standard of living enjoyed by the wealthiest residents at the end of the nineteenth century. The Union army officer made his fortune after the Civil War as a manufacturer of railroad freight cars and other profitable enterprises.

For this home, completed in 1892 in the French Renaissance style, Louis Kamper looked to royal digs in France's Loire Valley for inspiration, specifically Château de Chenonceau. The architect oversaw the exterior and interior design of the three-story, forty-nine-room, limestone-clad house with a pitched slate roof whose lavish interior finishes included wood-paneled rooms, elaborate parquet floors, marble- and onyx-clad fireplaces, a grand staircase and a twelve-foot-tall stained-glass window hanging in the landing and visible from Ferry Street. Even the carriage house encompassing over five thousand square feet is a spectacle.

Following Colonel Hecker's death, the mansion became a rooming house, apartment building, Smiley Brothers Music Company and law office before its purchase by Wayne State University for use as an alumni hall.

Charles Lang Freer, Hecker's younger business partner, opted for a more informal look next door at 71 East Ferry with his shingled, twenty-two-room cottage designed by noted Philadelphia architect Wilson Eyre Jr. Combining elements of the Queen Anne style, inspired by the Elizabethan cottage as a modern response to the ornate Victorian, and preeminent architect Henry Hobson Richardson's preference for stained shingles and rough stone, this house is considered one of the finest examples of cedar shake–style architecture in Michigan.

Many original features of the house were considered innovative at the time, such as electric wiring throughout, natural wood paneling, storage built-ins, bookshelves covering entire walls, cedar-lined drawers and a covered passageway connecting the carriage house and main house. An elevator carried wood from the basement to aid in supplying the dozen fireplaces. Design features included a lofty two-story foyer, arched entries, skylights and woven staircase balusters instead of spindles. It's believed Freer himself created the stain that was applied to the paneled walls and the ceiling beams.

The radical new residence built when Freer was in his early thirties might have raised eyebrows at the time of construction, according to *Detroit Free Press* staff writer Lilian Jackson Braun in her 1967 article, "Freer Home: Last Word in an Era of Riches." She wrote that the millionaire and "individualist" built the home to reflect his personal taste and probably didn't give "a split-shingle for anyone's opinion."

An avid art collector, Freer acquired more than 9,420 art objects and manuscripts before his death. His passion for Asian art evolved into one of the finest private collections, as did his interest in the works by the artist James McNeill Whistler. The devotee even purchased the acclaimed Whistler-designed dining room of a London residence called the *Peacock Room* and had it reinstalled in his Ferry Street home. Freer gifted the nation his amazing art collection, along with the funds to construct a building and an endowment fund for future studies and acquisitions. The Freer Gallery of Art opened on May 9, 1923, in Washington, D.C. It's the first museum at the Smithsonian dedicated exclusively to fine arts collections.

The Merrill-Palmer Skillman Institute, a national leader in childhood education since 1920, occupies the house today. It was purchased from the Freer estate with funds bequeathed by noted local philanthropist Lizzie Pitts Palmer.

Inventive tactics were employed to circumvent discriminatory real estate covenants in place until the 1940s that prevented black residents from owning property on the first two blocks of Ferry Street east of Woodward Avenue. The address of contractor William Lennane's corner home was changed in 1941 from 326 East Ferry to 5461 Brush Street when the Detroit Association of Women's Clubs, a black women's organization, purchased the property from the Lennane heirs and relocated the front door to Brush Street where no such restrictions existed. The original Ferry Street front entry was covered permanently in 1976 after a fire broke out in the clubhouse. The Detroit Association of Women's Clubs still owns the building.

5. DETROIT HISTORICAL MUSEUM

5401 Woodward Avenue

This must-visit museum chronicles Detroit's history from the 1700s to recent years through a variety of informative and interactive exhibits. Three newer galleries focus on Detroit's history of innovation and culture and its role as the "Arsenal of Democracy." The Kid Rock Music Lab, a popular exhibit, recounts Detroit's legendary music history, and the cobblestoned Streets of Old Detroit exhibit allows visitors to step back in time to experience life in early Detroit.

Whether your favorite type of history leans toward frontier, manufacturing, prominent people, sports, cars, fashion, politics or more, you'll uncover it all here as it relates to Detroit. Don't forget to check out the Legends Plaza outdoors in front of the building, where you'll find the handprints of Detroit legends such as Gordie Howe, Martha Reeves and Lily Tomlin.

Admission is free; the museum is closed on Mondays.

6. PARK SHELTON

15 East Kirby Street

The Park Shelton condominiums opened in 1926 as the Wardell apartment hotel built by former real estate auctioneer and Eureka Vacuum Company founder Fred Wardell. Ironically, Wardell's hotel is on Kirby Street.

Leasing phase advertisements in Detroit newspapers described the extended stay–style hotel as "the best home address in Detroit." The twelve-story posh residence "towering above Detroit's beautiful Art Center, and only ten minutes from downtown," answered one of the compelling "questions of the hour in Detroit today, 'Where shall we dine?'" The hotel featured a "popularly priced" coffee shop, bakery and "magnificent" dining room. Hotel residents could even serve up delicious meals, prepared by hotel chefs, in the privacy of their own apartments.

Other amenities included built-in electric ranges, dishwashers, refrigeration, Servidor service, maids, valets and ample garage facilities a short block away. Another popular feature— no inside apartments—meant residents enjoyed "abundant light and air everywhere."

Prominent guests included artist Diego Rivera, who lived here for about a year while he completed the Detroit Industry murals at the DIA, according to author Patricia Ibbottson in *Detroit's Historic Hotels and Restaurants*. Comedians Bob Hope, George Burns and Gracie Allen and actor Raymond Burr resided here when making local appearances.

7. DETROIT PUBLIC LIBRARY

5201 Woodward Avenue

In 1910, industrialist and philanthropist Andrew Carnegie donated $750,000 toward the city's library system, and it was decided a new main library would be built with the funds. Noted architect Cass Gilbert won the national competition held in 1912 to design it; however, construction of this three-story, Italian Renaissance–style masterpiece was put on hold when World War I broke out, delaying the opening until March 1921.

The library is the first building composing what's now known as the Cultural Center Historic District, which also includes the DIA and Rackham

Adam Strohm Hall, inside main Detroit Public Library, features colorful painted-glass windows and murals. *Man's Mobility* by John Stephens Coppins is visible in the distance. *Rod Arroyo*.

Building. The impetus behind the cultural center was Detroit's forty-fourth mayor, Philip Breitmayer, who had attended the 1893 Columbian Exposition in Chicago, where the City Beautiful movement began. This North American architecture and urban planning philosophy embraced the incorporation of beautification and monumental grandeur in city design. Brietmayer established a City Plan and Improvement Committee led by Frank Day of Philadelphia and Edward Bennett of Chicago. Daniel Burnham served as a

This vintage postcard depicts the Cass Gilbert–designed Detroit Public Library, dedicated in 1921. The beautiful main library is a Detroit must-see. *Author's collection.*

consultant. The stately library with its vast lawn and grand statuary reflects the pleasing aesthetic of the City Beautiful movement.

The exterior is constructed of Vermont marble and Serpentine Italian marble, and the phrase "Knowledge is Power" was carved into the marble above the main entrance on Woodward Avenue.

In addition to the sheer number of books and rare special collections held here, the library is known for its beautiful art. The murals and painted-glass windows in the Strohm gallery are a must-see.

8. DETROIT INSTITUTE OF ARTS (DIA)

5200 Woodward Avenue

The public dubbed this gorgeous Beaux-Arts building the "temple of art" when it opened in 1927. Today, it's ranked among the top six art museums in the nation and features a diverse collection of over sixty thousand works from around the globe ranging in scope from prehistory to the twenty-first century.

The museum began when *Detroit News* advertising manager William H. Brearly organized an art exhibit in 1883 to correlate with a popular newspaper series and published book that covered the five-month European travels of James E. Scripps, the newspaper's publisher and founder. Two years later, the Detroit Museum of Art was incorporated, and the first museum opened. Wealthy benefactors, including Scripps, donated valuable works of art by European masters to the fledgling museum. Fundraising efforts began in 1919 to build a new facility to house the museum's growing collection, and the name was changed to Detroit Institute of Arts.

German-born Wilhelm (William) Valentiner was hired to oversee the museum and served as director from 1924 to 1945. He's credited with developing the museum into one of the country's leading art institutions. His knowledge, extensive contacts in Europe and generous support from patrons enabled the scholar and art historian "to acquire many important works that established the framework of today's collections."

"Valentiner's tenure at Detroit included acquisitions of Pre-Columbian and African art, the first American museum to do so," states the Directory of Art Historians. Vincent van Gogh's *Self Portrait*, the first painting by the artist to be acquired by an American art museum, and Diego Rivera's *Detroit Industry*, which Rivera considered his most successful work, are two other notable acquisitions.

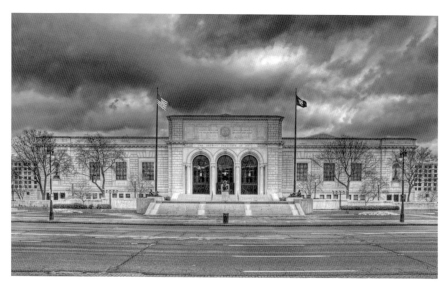

Detroit Institute of Arts, a cultural gem, houses one of the largest and most significant art collections in the nation. *Rod Arroyo.*

The *Detroit Industry* fresco in the Diego Court took eleven months to complete. While contemporary viewers marvel at what many consider the finest example of Mexican mural art in the United States, the reaction at its 1933 unveiling had the opposite effect. Many found the images by Rivera, a self-proclaimed Marxist, an affront to industry rather than a contemporary tribute to manufacturing and labor. Rivera's daring to question the role of industry in society and its influence on politics and class wasn't the only issue people had.

People also objected to the depiction of different races working side by side and called the nudes pornography, wrote Don Gonyea in a 2009 article for NPR: "One panel was labeled blasphemous by some members of the religious community. The section depicts a nativity scene where a baby is receiving a vaccination from a doctor and scientists from different countries took the place of the wise men." Religious leaders and community members embarked on a crusade to whitewash the murals. Supporters responded with their own passionate plea to keep the murals.

Edsel Ford, son of auto magnate Henry Ford, commissioned the work and initially remained aloof to the controversy, former DIA director Graham W.J. Beal said in a 2010 talk at the University of California–Berkeley Center for Latin American Studies. Ford later spoke out in support of the murals: "I am thoroughly convinced that the day will come when Detroit will be proud to have this work in its midst. In the years to come, they will be ranked among the truly great art treasures of America." He later released a statement through the Detroit Art Commission stating, "I admire Rivera's spirit. I really believe he was trying to express his idea of the spirit of Detroit."

The uproar may have died after that statement, but not the drama. According to Beal, many suspect Edsel Ford manufactured the controversy. Fred Black, who had worked directly for Ford, revealed many years later that Ford had been instructed to do something to convince city council it needed to act to renew waning public interest in the museum. Because of the Depression, the museum's $400,000 budget had been slashed to $40,000, and the Arts Commission voted to dismiss curators and educators. Ford stepped in and personally paid their salaries to keep the museum running.

Black claimed Ford's staff fed information about the murals to the right people, including clergy. Not only did the story break in Detroit papers, but it also made news around the world. When Black showed Ford the news accounts, most of the time he laughed and thought it was a great scheme.

"The end result was that city council voted to replace some of the museum's funding, thereby relieving Edsel Ford of having to pay everyone's salary," said Beal. "And so it is possible that the final act of exploitation in

Kresge Court at the DIA with a portion of the *Detroit Industry* fresco cycle by Diego Rivera in the background. *Rod Arroyo.*

this saga was that the Great Patron of Detroit arts, Edsel Ford himself, used Rivera and his murals to get people to come back to the museum and to reestablish its funding."

According to Beal, Ford paid Rivera almost $21,000 for his services, and Rivera was responsible for paying his workers. Twenty years after Henry Ford implemented the $5-per-day wage for unskilled workers, Rivera paid his four main assistants $12 a week. One assistant threatened to march in front of the museum saying Rivera was unfair to labor if he didn't get a raise. Rivera acquiesced. Other workers didn't receive any compensation. They were instructed to barter, or trade their sketches, to cover basic necessities and other needs. While Rivera used assistants to prepare the walls, he painted everything himself.

Art supplies were furnished by the museum, and the French cobalt blue pigment made from crushed lapis lazuli, a bright blue semi-precious stone mined for its intense color, was rather pricey at twenty-two dollars a pound.

The museum's classic white marble exterior representing the best of the Beaux-Arts style is also a work of art and garnered French-born architect Paul Philippe Cret (pronounced Cray) the prestigious 1928 Medal of Honor of the Architectural League of New York for his design.

The ornate 1,200-seat auditorium, now home to the Detroit Film Theatre, was a collaboration between Cret, who trained at the prestigious École des Beaux-Arts in Paris, and well-known local theater architect C. Howard Crane. The magnificent pipe organ built by Casavant Freres featured prominently in the design, as did the gorgeous two-story reception space flanked with crystal-reflecting end walls that bounce light off the elegantly arched windows and chandeliers. Wrought-iron interior grills by master blacksmith Samuel Yellin and terra-cotta tiles from Pewabic Pottery epitomized the exceptional craftsmanship of this era.

Renowned architect Gunnar Birkerts designed two bold, modern additions in 1966 and 1971 that contrasted starkly with the original museum. During an early 2000 six-year renovation and expansion project that he oversaw, architect Michael Graves reclad the additions with the same Danby marble from Vermont originally used by Cret.

Visitors frequently ask if Detroit almost lost its art during the city's bankruptcy proceedings. DIA supporters raised $100 million during an aggressive fundraising campaign to offset Detroit pension obligations as part of the city's bankruptcy exit plan, called the Grand Bargain. In turn, the DIA was granted nonprofit status and no longer subject to municipal financial woes.

For pertinent visitor information, please visit dia.org.

9. SCARAB CLUB

217 Farnsworth Street

The club promoting visual, auditory and literary arts dates to 1907, when a group of artists and art lovers met regularly to socialize and discuss art. In addition to painters, sculptors and other fine artists, members included automotive designers, graphic artists, photographers and architects. Club history indicates the name "Scarab Club" was adopted in 1913. The name was inspired by then president James Swan's collection of Egyptian scarabs, which symbolize resurrection of life.

From 1917 until 1950, the club hosted annual costume balls that were the highlight of Detroit's social season. Scarabean Cruise, the theme of the 1937 ball, was featured in *Life* magazine.

The beautiful Arts and Crafts clubhouse, which houses social areas, galleries and studios, was designed by architect and member Lancelot Sukert and opened in 1928. Of special note are the ceiling beams of the second-floor lounge, which have been signed by over two hundred artists who have walked through the doors over the past century, such as Diego Rivera, Marshall Fredericks and Norman Rockwell.

10. CHARLES H. WRIGHT MUSEUM OF AFRICAN AMERICAN HISTORY

315 East Warren Avenue

Until the recent opening of the National Museum of African American History in Washington, D.C., the Charles Wright Museum was the largest African American museum in the world. Its humble roots began in 1965, when Dr. Charles Wright, a local obstetrician and gynecologist, partnered with over thirty local organizations and established Detroit's first International Afro-American Museum.

Inspired by a memorial to Danish World War II heroes he had visited on a recent trip to Denmark, Dr. Wright believed African Americans needed a similar center to document, preserve and educate the public on their history, life and culture.

The small collection of African masks, Elijah McCoy inventions and other artifacts increased over the years, and the museum outgrew its first location.

Ten years after moving to the second location, this beautiful, state-of-the-art 125,000-square-foot facility opened in April 1997.

The Ford Freedom Rotunda is a light-filled space featuring a glass dome larger in size than our state capitol building. Ninety-two flags ring the rotunda, representing countries involved in the Atlantic slave trade from which most African Americans descend. *Ring of Genealogy*, a moving thirty-seven-foot terrazzo mosaic by Hubert Massey installed in the center floor, depicts the black experience in America. Nameplates engraved with the names of prominent African Americans surround the creation.

The museum's premier exhibit is the twenty-two-thousand-square-foot And Still We Rise: Our Journey Through African American History and Culture, where life-size wax figures of men, women and children tell the story of the intolerable conditions of the slave trade. The exhibit includes a model of a slave ship.

Sims Varner & Associates was the architectural firm commissioned to design the museum. When Harold Varner, firm partner and architect on the design team, died in December 2014, his daughter Kimberly Varner Tandy told the Associated Press it was an honor for her father to design the museum: "The rotunda is an example of things he had experienced as we travelled to Africa. He wanted it to be more of a gathering place than a museum. That's what he was trying to impart into that building, a place to come and experience the culture as well as celebrate our heritage."

The museum houses over thirty-five thousand artifacts, archival materials, a library and a theater. When civil rights pioneer Rosa Parks died in 2005 and Queen of Soul Aretha Franklin in 2018, visitation and memorial services were held here.

11. MACCABEES BUILDING

5057 Woodward Avenue

This Albert Kahn–designed fifteen-story skyscraper opened in 1927 as the headquarters for the fraternal organization Knights of Maccabees, which originated in London, Ontario, Canada, in the late nineteenth century. Currently owned by Wayne State University, the building is worth a visit for close-up views of the opulent architectural details found above exterior entrances, as well as the stunning interior mosaics covering the lobby ceiling and Art Deco light fixtures.

The Lone Ranger and Green Hornet, fictional characters of popular television series, movies and comic books, debuted as radio shows in the 1930s and were broadcast live from the WXYZ studio once located here.

12. WAYNE STATE UNIVERSITY

42 West Warren Avenue

Located in the heart of the city with access to all the nearby cultural gems, this urban university attracts students from all over the state, country and world. The school traces its beginnings to 1868 with the founding of Detroit Medical College, now the School of Medicine. In 1881, the Detroit Normal Training School was established and progressed into the School of Education. College classes offered at Central High School, now Old Main Hall, a WSU institution, evolved into the College of Liberal Arts and Sciences.

From this auspicious start, the university grew. Currently, over twenty-seven thousand students are enrolled in undergraduate, graduate and doctorate programs such as nursing, pharmacy, business, performing arts, law, education and social work. Wayne State University is nationally recognized for its excellence in research too.

The campus encompasses over two hundred acres and includes many notable buildings. The former high school, now Old Main, opened in 1896 and is a fine example of Romanesque Revival style. The Frederick Linsell and Max Jacob homes found on the main campus, now used by the university, pay homage to the wealthy neighborhood once located here during the early twentieth century. Four buildings designed by renowned architect Minoru Yamasaki can also be found on the main campus. They are the College of Education, MacGregor Conference Center and adjacent reflecting pool, Helen L. DeRoy Auditorium and the Prentis Building.

It's also worth a walk across campus to St. Andrews Episcopal Church. In the park in front of the church stand four ten-foot limestone statues representing French explorers and priests significant to Detroit and Michigan history: Antoine de la Mothe Cadillac, Robert de La Salle, Father Gabriel Richard and Father Jacques Marquette. The Julius Melchers sculptures originally adorned the Old City Hall, built in 1885 and demolished in 1960.

Another worthwhile stop is the Walter Reuther Library of Labor and Urban Affairs, the largest labor archive in North America.

13. CATHEDRAL CHURCH OF ST. PAUL

4800 Woodward Avenue

The Episcopal Diocese of Michigan and Parish of St. Paul is as gorgeous inside as out. Renowned Princeton architect Ralph Adams Cram designed this cathedral in 1911 in the Late Gothic Revival style popular then. In keeping true to early English Gothic construction techniques, Cram used flying buttresses and arched roofs for support instead of steel reinforcements. As fitting of a cathedral, inside you'll find soaring arches, elaborate wood carvings and stained-glass windows. Most of the glass windows were designed based on windows found in France and England from the thirteenth and fourteenth centuries. One exception is the brilliant colored window representing the Visit of the Magi. Created by Franz Mayer and Company of Munich, a well-known German glass maker, the window features life-sized figures.

The Parish of St. Paul dates back to 1824 and was the first Episcopal and Protestant congregation in the then Michigan Territory. On April 9, 1947,

Detroit-made Pewabic tiles are one of many beautiful architectural details found inside the Episcopal Diocese of Michigan's Cathedral Church of St. Paul. *Rod Arroyo.*

the funeral service for industrialist Henry Ford took place at the cathedral. Throngs of people gathered outside in the rain to pay their respects, as there was no room inside for all the mourners.

14. FIRST CONGREGATIONAL CHURCH OF DETROIT

33 Forest Avenue

While the congregation of "Historic First" originated on December 25, 1844, the third and present structure was built in 1891. Inspired by Italian ecclesiastical architecture found in Venice and Ravenna, Boston architect John Faxon incorporated grand ornamentation and symbolism in the church's design, which combines elements of Romanesque and Byzantine architectural styles.

Historic First's sanctuary rivals its European counterparts with its abundance of ornate carved wood, detailed ceiling portraits, beautiful rose windows and host of handcrafted details. The remarkable ceiling paintings of the four evangelists representing the four Gospels was done by French-trained artist Lyle Durgin of Boston. Durgin and her sister, Harriet, were well-known female artists at the time.

One of the largest and finest organs built by respected Canadian organ maker Casavant Freres of St. Hyacinthe, Quebec, was installed in the church in 1918 by Joseph Hebert. He rebuilt and restored the original instrument forty-two years later, according to church history.

The striking bell tower features an 8-foot-tall, two-hundred-pound copper likeness of the Archangel Uriel above its 120-foot-high base. The tower's elaborate door mimics the main door of the Cathedral of Pisa in Italy.

Celebrated Detroit architect Albert Kahn designed the 1925 community house addition, which includes a luxurious lounge and dining room, stage, gymnasium, offices and classrooms. In addition to worship and community outreach services, the beautiful Historic First is a popular wedding venue. The church is also known for its Underground Railroad Living Museum.

15. THE WHITNEY RESTAURANT

4421 Woodward Avenue

The grand homes of the late nineteenth century lining both sides of Woodward Avenue have long been replaced by commercial buildings. Luckily, one home, the grandest of them all, still stands. The Whitney, now an upscale restaurant, allows visitors an opportunity to enjoy dinner, drinks or dessert while basking in the grandeur of another era.

No expense was spared in the construction of this lavish mansion built for lumber baron David Whitney Jr. and his family. Whitney was one of the richest men in Detroit and the entire state at the time. Built in the Romanesque Revival style, the pink exterior was constructed from South Dakota jasper, and features include a grand front porch, second-floor balcony, turrets and magnificent bay windows. The interior doesn't disappoint either. The grand staircase makes quite an impression as soon as you walk through the door. Fifty-two well-appointed rooms, including ten bathrooms, occupy three floors. The mansion features twenty fireplaces and an elevator—the first home in the Midwest to have one! Finishes include rich carved wood, marble, precious metals and Tiffany stained-glass windows estimated to be worth more today than the entire house.

The commission for building this lavish mansion went to Gordon W. Lloyd, a prominent local architect who designed many local Episcopal churches, including Central United Methodist Church and Christ Church. Completed in 1894, it took four years to build and cost $400,000. The Whitney's website quotes an article in the February 4, 1894 edition of the *Detroit Free Press* stating, "The new home enjoys the distinction of being the most pretentious modern home in the state and one of the most elaborate houses in the West."

16. WEST CANFIELD HISTORIC DISTRICT

West Canfield Avenue between Second and Third Streets

This block of grand Queen Anne– and Victorian-style homes built in the 1870s exemplifies what the surrounding neighborhood once looked like.

A state historical marker reads:

In 1813, Territorial Governor Lewis Cass purchased the Macomb farm. By 1818 he had acquired "80 arpents in depth" of land extending almost three miles inland from the Detroit River in the form of a narrow French ribbon farm. Cass died in 1866. In 1869 his daughters Matilda Cass Ledyard and Mary Cass Canfield subdivided block 98 and donated 100 feet for an avenue which they named Canfield in memory of Mary's husband, Captain Augustus Canfield. Lewis Cass, Jr. subdivided block 100 on the north side of Canfield in 1871. Many of Detroit's most prominent attorneys, physicians, dentists and architects owned homes on West Canfield. In the 1880s, the area became commonly known as Piety Hill because of the alleged social and moral character of its residents.

A prime residential area for Detroit's wealthy residents for decades, the neighborhood began to decline in the 1930s with the onset of the Great Depression. An influx of multi-family residences built to accommodate the growing labor force also played a role. As the area became more commercial, many of the beautiful homes were demolished. In the 1960s, a group of residents organized to preserve this important piece of Detroit history. They even hauled granite pavers from an old section of Atwater Street, which now is below the Renaissance Center, to re-create a charming old cobbled road.

17. ORCHESTRA HALL

3711 Woodward Avenue

Home of the Detroit Symphony Orchestra (DSO), the beautiful music hall was built at the request of then music director Ossip Gabrilowitsch. The famous pianist refused to extend his contract unless a new hall was built. The DSO played its first concert in the new home on October 23, 1919. Known for having the best acoustics in the country, the Detroit Symphony Orchestra broadcasted a performance live from the hall over the radio station WWJ-AM, becoming the first radio broadcast of a symphony orchestra.

An interior view of Orchestra Hall, built to the specifications of the Detroit Symphony Orchestra's founding director, Ossip Gabrilowitsch. *Courtesy of Library of Congress.*

Corktown · Sites of Interest

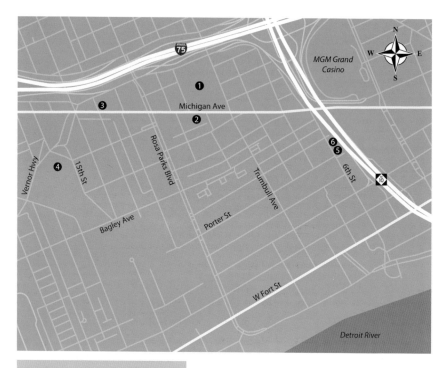

1. Former Tiger Stadium
2. Former Carhartt Factory
3. Gaelic League
4. Michigan Central Station
5. Most Holy Trinity Church
6. Workers Row House

CHAPTER 4

CORKTOWN

Settled by the Irish working class in the 1850s, Corktown, named for County Cork in Ireland, is one of Detroit's oldest neighborhoods. Although Irish immigrants came to America as early as Revolutionary War times, the first mass wave of Irish immigrants came in the early 1800s and settled in the East. Detroit was still a frontier village and held no great appeal. Since the East Coast population was predominantly Protestant, clashes between Irish Catholic immigrants and Protestant residents became common. When the Erie Canal opened in 1825, Catholic Detroit drew many of the immigrants west.

The next influx of immigrants came to Detroit and other North American cities following the Great Famine or Great Hunger of 1845, which occurred when blight struck potato crops, a staple crop grown in rural Ireland. Poor harvests over three consecutive years led to the death of one million Irish citizens and the exodus of one million to North America or England.

Residents of Corktown today are proud of their Irish heritage and continue to carry on many of the traditions these immigrants brought with them.

1. TIGER STADIUM

2121 Trumbull Avenue

The corner of Trumbull and Michigan Avenues, now home to the Detroit Police Athletic League headquarters and Willie Horton Field of Dreams youth sports facility, is hallowed ground for Detroit Tigers baseball fans of a certain age. It's here that the venerated Tiger Stadium once stood and baseball magic occurred.

The Detroit Tigers played at this location since 1896, when it was called Bennett Park and they were a minor-league baseball team. In 1901, the Detroit Tigers team became a charter member of the American League, and the rest is history.

Although the stadium would undergo many expansions, owners and name changes (Navin Field, Briggs Stadium, Tiger Stadium), the Detroit Tigers would call this place home for over a century. Here they would clinch the American League pennant nine times and go on to win the World Championship four times (1935, 1945, 1968, 1984). It was "the corner" where Detroit Tigers legends such as Ty Cobb, Goose Goslin, Mickey Cochrane, Mickey Lolich, Al Kaline, Kirk Gibson, Willie Horton, Gates Brown, Mark Fidrych, Lou Whittaker, Alan Trammel and Jim Northrup played.

The mere mention of this revered ballpark evokes passionate memories from fans invoking all the senses. They fondly recall seats so close to the action where you felt like you were part of the game because you could hear the conversations between the players on the field. For some, player access

Legendary baseball player Tyrus "Ty" Cobb spent twenty-two seasons with the Detroit Tigers. He's featured on a 1912 American Tobacco trading card alongside team manager Hugh Jennings. *Courtesy of Library of Congress.*

An era of baseball history ended with the demolition of Tiger Stadium, tied with Boston's Fenway Park as the oldest Major League Baseball ballpark when it closed. *Rod Arroyo.*

was incredible, evoking vivid memories of working at nearby restaurants and delivering sandwiches to the players during practices. The players would then often take a minute to sign autographs. They recall the spectacle of witnessing Reggie Jackson hit a home run off the roof of the right light tower during the 1971 All-Star game or the deafening but euphoric sound made when fans seated in the bleachers cheered, jeered and stomped their feet. Even the smell was magical, said one fan. "If you shut your eyes, you knew you were at Tiger Stadium."

The ballpark was also home to football. The Detroit Lions played at "the corner" from 1938 to 1974. Major concerts by performers such as the Three Tenors, Rod Stewart and Kiss were held here. In June 1990, South African anti-apartheid leader Nelson Mandela spoke before a crowd of nearly fifty thousand. Mandela, who had just been released after spending twenty-seven years in a South African prison, visited eight American cities, including Detroit, as part of his Freedom Tour.

The final game at this historic site was played on September 27, 1999. Over 102 million fans passed through the ballpark's turnstiles between 1912 and 1999. When the park closed, it was tied with Boston's Fenway Park as the oldest stadium in Major League Baseball. A decade after closing, Tiger Stadium was demolished.

2. FORMER CARHARTT FACTORY

1623 Michigan Avenue (approximate vicinity)

San Francisco may lay claim to the Levi Strauss & Co. invention known today as blue jeans, but Detroit is where Carhartt, the iconic work clothing label, originated. In 1889, Hamilton Carhartt & Company was established after its founder, Hamilton Carhartt, began making sturdy work clothes for railroad employees. Business boomed, and the fledgling venture, which began with two sewing machines and five employees, grew to meet the demand. The company's first and only Detroit factory was located on Michigan Avenue between Tenth and Eleventh Streets. Bucharest Grill, a popular local restaurant chain famous for its chicken schwarma, sits close to where the factory once stood.

According to Carhartt archivist Dave J. Moore, the original factory opened around 1893 and underwent expansion in later years. Work clothes were manufactured locally until 1932, when operations moved to Irvine, Kentucky, where garments are still produced today. After remaining vacant for a decade, the former factory was demolished.

Early Carhartt advertisement touting its state-of-the-art Detroit factory, where annual garment production exceeded two million and workers enjoyed eight-hour days. *Courtesy of Carhartt.*

Vintage Carhartt advertisement pays tribute to its humble roots outfitting railroad workers and its reliance on union-made clothing. *Courtesy of Carhartt.*

An apparel staple for the trades for over one hundred years, Carhartt found a new audience and became a global fashion sensation in the later twentieth and early twenty-first centuries after punk, grunge and hip-hop artists sported the work wear.

While the Carhartt brand is no longer manufactured in Detroit, its corporate headquarters is located in the nearby suburb of Dearborn, also home to Ford Motor Company. In August 2015, Carhartt returned to its Detroit roots with the opening of a unique flagship retail store at 5800 Cass Avenue.

The Carhartt family continues to make important contributions to Detroit. Gretchen Valade, granddaughter of Carhartt founder Hamilton Carhartt, established an arts endowment in her name. She donated $15 million to the Detroit Jazz Festival and $9.5 million to Wayne State University for the creation of the Gretchen Valade Jazz Center.

3. GAELIC LEAGUE OF DETROIT IRISH AMERICAN CLUB

2068 Michigan Avenue

Visitors of this popular Irish American social club are immediately put at ease by the affable Irish greeting *Céad míle fáilte,* or one hundred thousand welcomes. Although the club's origin dates back to 1920, its mission of promoting the "common welfare and culture of the Irish race in Detroit and elsewhere" remains unchanged even today. While members are welcome to sip pints in the pub, the club offers a variety of cultural activities and lessons, such as Sunday square dances or Ceili dancing, a popular form of Irish folk dancing; Irish language circles; Celtic harp lessons; and music performances by well-known Irish entertainers and local musicians. The club even hosts its own Irish radio show.

Members promote the Corktown community by taking on leadership roles in major events such as the annual home tour and St. Patrick's Day parade, a long-standing, enormously popular event where everyone dons green and is Irish.

Do you have to be Irish to join the club? Anyone eighteen years of age or older who possesses good moral character can join the Irish American Club. Annual dues are twenty dollars. Gaelic League membership, however, requires Irish birth or ancestry. In order to be considered for Gaelic League membership, candidates must first be active and contributing members of the Irish American Club for twenty-four consecutive months. Gaelic League members possess voting rights.

4. MICHIGAN CENTRAL STATION

2001 Fifteenth Street

Michigan Central Station is probably one of the most recognizable Detroit buildings. For the past decade, this once majestic building has been the site of a ruin porn feeding frenzy, with photographs of the building in its derelict state published in books, blogs, newspapers and social media and portrayed as a symbol of a great industrial city's decline. These authors and photographers frequently failed to mention that the building has been privately owned since 1996 by one of Michigan's wealthiest men. So is the train station's demise really representative of Detroit's decline or more indicative of weak redevelopment laws that allow speculators to hold on to buildings for decades without doing much to improve them?

Rail travel reached its height during the First World War, which spanned from 1914 to 1918. To keep up with the demand, a new passenger station was needed in Detroit. "New Depot Is One of Finest in Country," according to the December 27, 1913 *Detroit Free Press*. Construction began in June 1912, and the unfinished station was rushed into early service on December 26, 1913, when a fire swept through the original train station located on Fort Street being replaced by Michigan Central Station.

Built at the same time as New York's Grand Central Station and using the same architectural firms of Warren and Wetmore and Reed and Stern, both stations were similar in style and meant to be flagship stations on the Vanderbilt-owned rail line. The exterior was done in a classical style with Beaux-Arts elements. The opulent interior of the passenger terminal, designed to replicate a Roman bathhouse, sported vaulted ceilings, marble walls, Greek columns and a copper skylight. There were eleven tracks for the use of passenger trains, and the longest held a "train of 18 Pullman cars under cover." Besides the waiting room in the concourse on the main floor, there was a reading room for men, a tearoom, a restaurant, a lunchroom, a barbershop and a drugstore. A few of the notable passengers who passed through the doors included Presidents Herbert Hoover, Harry

Image of the legendary Michigan Central Station taken a few years ago, with *The Cornfield* mural by local artist Vito Valdez in the foreground. Photos of the imposing railroad station were flaunted by writers and photographers worldwide as a symbol of Detroit's decline. *Rod Arroyo.*

Truman and Franklin Roosevelt; actor Charlie Chaplin; and inventor Thomas Edison.

The second part of the design included an attached, eighteen-story office structure built behind the passenger terminal. Originally, the offices were supposed to house a hotel and the corporate offices of Michigan Central Station. The hotel never materialized, and Michigan Central occupied only a few floors for corporate use.

Michigan Central Station had a few strikes against it from the beginning. It was located outside the central business district with the intent of spurring development in the area. That development never occurred. After World War I, the death knell for train travel sounded as automobiles began to replace trains as the preferred transportation method, especially in Detroit. With Detroit playing a pivotal role in arms manufacturing during World War II, train travel increased locally as the station was used to deploy soldiers and move military equipment and weapons. After the war, train travel declined rapidly as more people owned cars. Airline travel became more affordable for ordinary citizens as well. Service was cut back. The 1960s saw the closure of the restaurant and shops. In 1971, Amtrak took over the station and provided service through January 1988. From 1988 until 1996, Michigan Central became a hot spot to hold rave parties and a prime destination for scrappers and illegal urban explorers. During this time, building ownership changed multiple times, with most investors short of the necessary cash to underwrite a renovation of this size. City officials entertained the idea of relocating the police headquarters here as well as demolishing the station.

After sitting vacant for decades, the privately owned building was sold to Ford Motor Company in early 2018 to be used as the headquarters for its autonomous car division. Thousands of people showed up to tour the building over several weekends when the automotive giant opened it to the public.

5. MOST HOLY TRINITY CHURCH

1050 Porter Street

The need for an English-language Catholic church in Detroit arose in the 1830s due to an influx of Irish immigrants. When no Irish priest was available to take the post, Father Martin Kundig, a twenty-three-year-old German and former member of the Vatican Swiss Guard, organized the church. In August 1834, he purchased a former Protestant meetinghouse located at Woodward Avenue and Larned Street and moved it to Cadillac Square and Bates.

A cholera epidemic swept through the city before the church could be consecrated, and the building was converted into the Michigan Territory's first hospital. Twenty-eight women served as nurses and fourteen men as physicians. Thus began what the church calls its "legacy of service." Ten months later, on Trinity Sunday, Most Holy Trinity Church was dedicated.

In 1848, the new Saints Peter and Paul Jesuit Church located at Jefferson Avenue and St. Antoine absorbed the congregation into its fold, leaving former parishioners unhappy with this new arrangement. The following year, they reestablished their church and moved the original meetinghouse to Porter Street. As the parish grew, plans for a new church were drawn. Irish-born Patrick C. Keely, a distinguished architect of Catholic churches at the time, designed the Gothic Revival church, and its cornerstone was laid on October 28, 1855.

Throughout the years, the church has undergone extensive remodeling and redecorating and the addition of a school and rectory. The organ still in use today dates back to 1867. Built by German immigrant Andreas Moeller, the organ relies on trackers, a system of levers and wooden strips, instead of electricity to push air through the pipes and create sound. It's believed to be the oldest Michigan-built organ still in use in its original location and the oldest in Detroit.

Tragedy befell the parish on July 22, 1880, when 12 altar boys and their 5 chaperones drowned in the Detroit River during an annual outing to Monroe, Michigan. The excursion steamer *Garland*, with 1,200 passengers aboard, collided with the steam yacht *Mamie* at 10:00 p.m., cutting it in two. A bronze plaque hangs in remembrance inside the church.

6. WORKERS ROW HOUSE

1430 Sixth Street

Detroit's "Eighth Ward," as it was called in the 1840s and 1850s, saw a large influx of working-class immigrants. Most resided in cramped tenement housing such as this example built in 1849. This two-story structure housed three adjacent 560-square-foot units, each equipped with one bedroom and a sleeping loft. It wasn't uncommon to find a dozen adults sharing one unit and rotating sleeping quarters based on work shifts.

Recent archaeological digs by students from Wayne State University and University of Michigan–Flint have unearthed a treasure-trove of household items, shedding light on the early history of the building and its residents.

MORE THAN CARS:
OTHER PROMINENT INDUSTRIES

1. The Caille Brothers Company, a leader in the slot machine and novelty industry from 1895 to 1937, operated the largest plant in the world devoted exclusively to their production.
2. Burroughs Adding Machine Company became one of the largest adding machine companies in America.
3. Hollywood may be the motion picture capital, but Detroit was home to the industrial film industry. The Jam Handy Organization produced thousands of instructional films for the armed forces, education and businesses, including Coca-Cola and Chevrolet. *Rudolph the Red-Nosed Reindeer*, written by Robert Lewis May, made its screen debut in 1948 as a cartoon short produced by Max Fleischer and Jam Handy Corporation.
4. Detroit Publishing Company was a major worldwide image publisher from 1895 to 1924 producing prints of landscapes and city scenes around the world for resale as postcards, colored photographs and lantern slides.
5. Parke-Davis and Company, a leading pharmaceutical firm established in the 1870s, built the nation's first industrial pharmaceutical research laboratory.

Belle Isle Park & Nearby Sites of Interest

1. **Belle Isle Park**
   a. MacArthur Bridge
   b. Detroit Boat Club
   c. Sunset Point
   d. Scott Memorial Fountain
   e. Casino
   f. Dossin Great Lakes Museum
   g. Anna Scripps Whitcomb Conservatory
   h. Aquarium
   i. US Coast Guard Station
   j. Livingstone Memorial Lighthouse
   k. Detroit Yacht Club
   l. Public Beach

2. **Gold Coast**
3. **Indian Village**
4. **Joseph Berry Subdivision/ Manoogian Mansion**
5. **Waterworks Park**
6. **Pewabic Pottery**

CHAPTER 5

BELLE ISLE PARK AND NEARBY SITES OF INTEREST

1. BELLE ISLE PARK

East Grand Boulevard and Jefferson Avenue

A Detroit jewel, this 2.5-mile-long, 987-acre island park, located in the international waters of the Detroit River, is owned by the City of Detroit, making it the largest city-owned island park in the nation. Since it is managed by the Michigan Department of Natural Resources under a thirty-year lease as part of the city's financial restructuring, it's also the 102nd state park.

Offering up approximately seven miles of shoreline, Belle Isle is a picturesque spot. While nearly a third of the island is a natural wooded area and home to a wide variety of small animals and birds, the park also features ample recreational opportunities, including a public beach and many historic public landmarks and monuments.

The island has a unique ecology, according to the Belle Isle Conservancy. "More than half of the island is covered by three lakes, a lagoon and 230 acres of forested wetlands. Its rare wet-mesic forest contains specimens that mimic the Detroit ecosystem of hundreds of years ago."

The services of Frederick Law Olmsted, the leading landscape architect of the post–Civil War era whose prominent commissions included New York's Central Park, were enlisted to create a design that would put Belle Isle on par with the country's premier parks. Only a few elements of his plan were implemented, such as a pedestrian-friendly Central Avenue and combination pavilion/ferry landing.

Prior to its development as a park in the mid-nineteenth century, Belle Isle served as a commons area where early settlers kept their pigs safe from marauding wolves. Brothers Frank and Arthur Woodford wrote in their local history *All Our Yesterdays* that Ile aux Cochons, or Hog Island, was the island's name.

Before air conditioning became a staple in most homes, old photos show residents escaping the insufferable summer heat by spreading blankets on the lush grass and sleeping outdoors at the park.

A. MacArthur Bridge

This picturesque bridge has connected the island to the mainland since it opened on November 1, 1923, replacing an iron bridge with wood decking destroyed by fire in April 1915. Originally named for our nation's first president, George Washington, the bridge was renamed in 1942 to honor five-star American general Douglas MacArthur, best known for his command of Allied forces in the Pacific Theater during World War II.

The original iron bridge was the site of two well-known exploits. On Tuesday, November 27, 1906, master illusionist Harry Houdini jumped from the bridge while shackled, freeing himself from the handcuffs while submerged underwater. The jump is one of Houdini's most well-known acts because he continually embellished the details of his dramatic escape each time he told the story. In 1913, William E. Scripps, son of *Detroit News* founder James E. Scripps, flew a plane under the bridge. Scripps was the first man in Michigan to own and fly a plane.

Prior to the construction of either bridge, guests accessed the island park via ferries or excursion boats departing from downtown docks.

Douglas MacArthur Bridge, named for the five-star general and World War II hero, provides access to Belle Isle, the city's popular island park. *Rod Arroyo.*

B. DETROIT BOAT CLUB

The Detroit Boat Club was organized on February 18, 1839, making it the first boat club in North America and one of the oldest continuously operating rowing organizations in the world. The current boathouse was completed in 1902 and sits on the site of two previous boathouses destroyed by fire. Fundraising efforts are underway to restore the clubhouse.

Image of the current Detroit Boat Club taken by a Detroit Publishing Company photographer in 1905. Founded in 1839, it's the oldest boat club in the United States. *Courtesy of Library of Congress.*

C. SUNSET POINT

This picnic area at the western tip of the island offers some of the best views of the Detroit skyline and is a spot frequented by amateur and professional photographers.

D. JAMES SCOTT MEMORIAL FOUNTAIN

Downtown building sites provided the two hundred acres of fill used to expand the western part of the island in 1915 to accommodate this beautiful fountain and lake. After a national competition was held, architect Cass Gilbert received the commission to design the impressive Vermont white marble fountain, which rivals those found in Europe. Dedicated on May 31, 1925, the popular attraction and backdrop for wedding photos features stacking bowls and over one hundred delightful water spouts in shapes of lions, turtles and Neptune figures.

A likeness of the fountain's benefactor and namesake can be found seated nearby. New York sculptor Herbert Adams designed the bronze statue of

The majestic James Scott Fountain on Belle Isle, a favorite local landmark, rivals beautiful fountains found elsewhere in the world. Its benefactor was considered by many to be a scoundrel. *Rod Arroyo.*

James Scott, a wealthy real estate speculator and gaming house proprietor, whose activities brought great scrutiny and criticism. So disliked was this guy that when he bequeathed the funds upon his death for the construction of a fountain, contingent upon including a life-sized statue of himself, civic and religious leaders balked. They eventually acquiesced when his already sizeable gift kept increasing and it was determined what a grand spectacle could be built with his funds.

E. CASINO

Designed by architects Van Leyen and Schilling, this attractive building with arched porticos spanning its length opened in 1908. It replaced an impressive three-story wooden structure destroyed by fire just a few years before. Although called a casino, the building was never a place for gambling. Instead, high-society members hosted fancy functions here. Elegant banks of doors and windows line the casino's north and south elevations. Not only did the windows provide beautiful views of the river and park, but they also kept the building and guests cool during the hot summer months when they were opened, allowing river breezes to flow through.

An early 1900s image of Belle Isle casino taken by Detroit Publishing Company. Ladies are sitting on the first-floor veranda while tuxedoed waiters serve diners on the second floor. *Courtesy of Library of Congress.*

F. DOSSIN GREAT LAKES MUSEUM

This sixteen-thousand-square-foot museum showcases the story of the Great Lakes with a special emphasis on Detroit's role in regional and national maritime history, from the shipping fleets that ruled the waterways to the influence of the Great Lakes and Detroit River in our region's industrial and social history.

The original City's Maritime Museum opened in 1949 aboard the landed wood schooner *J.T. Wing*, the last commercial sailing ship on the Great Lakes. By 1956, the deteriorating condition of the *J.T. Wing* forced the museum to close. A new museum opened on the same site on July 24, 1960, due to a generous donation from the Dossin family, avid hydroplane racers.

Popular exhibits include the *Miss Pepsi*, a championship hydroplane raced by the Dossin family in the 1950s; the massive bow anchor off the legendary *Edmund Fitzgerald*, which sank in Lake Superior; and the restored Gothic Room, or smoking lounge, from the SS *City of Detroit III*, a luxury steamship that plied the waters during the golden age of Great Lakes cruise ships.

From the SS *William Clay Ford* pilot house, visitors can "captain" one of the city's most noted freighters while enjoying prime views of the Detroit River. Both adults and children will enjoy the many hands-on and interactive exhibits found here.

G. ANNA SCRIPPS WHITCOMB CONSERVATORY

Exotic and rare plants from around the world are on display in the nation's oldest continuously operating conservatory, which opened on August 18, 1904. Like the aquarium next door, the original wood-frame building was designed by Albert Kahn. It was rebuilt with steel and aluminum mid-century.

Christened the Aquarium and Horticultural Building, it was renamed in 1955 in honor of Anna Scripps Whitcomb, daughter of *Detroit News* founder James Scripps, for her generous donation to the city of six hundred orchids from her personal collection.

Seasonal flower beds, manicured grounds and a koi-filled lily pond compose the thirteen acres occupied by the conservatory. Statuary accents on the grounds include the lovely Levi Barbour Memorial Fountain designed by Marshall Fredericks; a Japanese stone lantern gifted to the city in 1985 by a visiting delegation from Toyota, Japan; and a peacock sundial erected in 1927.

H. Aquarium

The Albert Kahn–designed aquarium also opened on August 18, 1904, making it the oldest aquarium in the nation. Clownfish, koi and pufferfishes are just a sampling of the more than one thousand fish on display at this favorite destination for generations of Detroiters.

The beloved Albert Kahn–designed Belle Isle Aquarium opened in 1904 and is the oldest aquarium in the United States. *Rod Arroyo.*

I. U.S. Coast Guard Station

The original Belle Isle lighthouse constructed for the U.S. Coast Guard shone its light for the first time on May 15, 1882. It was replaced in 1942 by the current station, the most modern facility on the Great Lakes at the time. The mooring basin, launch ways and boat-handling facilities were exceptional, and the watch tower was unparalleled. Round-the-clock surveillance of the Detroit River and Lake St. Clair was conducted in the seventy-five-foot tower using the most up-to-date equipment and instrumentation available at the time.

J. LIVINGSTONE MEMORIAL LIGHTHOUSE

Located at the north end of Belle Isle, the nation's only marble lighthouse was built with private donations as a memorial to William Livingstone, president of the Lake Carriers' Association from 1902 to 1925. Designed by Albert Kahn and featuring ornamental reliefs by Hungarian architect and sculptor Giza Maroti, the lighthouse began operating in 1930.

The white Georgia marble lighthouse on Belle Isle is a memorial to William Livingstone, a prominent local businessman best known for his contributions to Great Lakes shipping. *Rod Arroyo.*

K. DETROIT YACHT CLUB

Housed in a beautiful 1920s Mediterranean-style villa, the Detroit Yacht Club enjoys the claim of being the largest yacht club in the United States and the twelfth oldest. The private club was founded shortly after the end of the Civil War. A small clubhouse and sailing shed were built at the foot of McDougall Street, just south of Jefferson Avenue, in the late 1870s. The first clubhouse erected on Belle Isle in 1891 was destroyed by fire thirteen years later. A new million-dollar clubhouse designed by George Mason was erected immediately on the ashes of the old clubhouse and features grand staircases, an elaborate ballroom and an Olympic-sized indoor swimming pool lined with Pewabic tiles.

L. PUBLIC BEACH

The city's only public swimming beach is located on the island. Within minutes, one can leave work behind and relax on the half-mile sandy beach providing spectacular views of the downtown skyline or cool down by taking a refreshing dip in the water.

2. GOLD COAST

Jefferson Avenue East of East Grand Boulevard

The land along the Detroit River east of "the Boulevard" was attractive in the early 1920s to real estate developers who wanted to build a community of luxury apartments that would appeal to a sophisticated audience. Conveniently located just a few miles from downtown, the property was far enough away from the noise and pollution now ever-present in the growing city. The waterfront views overlooking beautiful Belle Isle provided the tranquil setting developers sought.

Wealthy residents, such as Edsel and Eleanor Ford, who lived in waterfront homes neighboring these proposed developments, weren't so enamored with the prospect of living next to large-scale commercial apartments. The Fords promptly hired architect Albert Kahn to design the lavish Ford estate that still stands today on Lake Shore Drive in nearby Grosse Pointe Shores. Once the Fords moved out, their house was demolished to make way for multi-family developments.

Today, you'll find an eclectic mix of architecture styles ranging from elegant 1920s Tudor to mid-century modern high-rises. One architectural standout is the recently renovated Alden Park Towers, which was built in 1923. (The Ford house was next door.) The Tudor Revival–style complex is composed of four connected brick towers, which gives it the appearance of a sprawling castle. It's hard to miss the ruins of Whittier Hotel looming in the background. The fifteen-story structure was built in the 1920s as an exclusive extended-stay hotel. First Lady Eleanor Roosevelt, Mae West, Frank Sinatra and the Beatles are a few of the noteworthy guests who stayed at the hotel. According to local lore, the manager of the Whittier cut the bedsheets allegedly used by Beatles members John, Paul, George and Ringo into small squares and sold them to fans as souvenirs.

3. INDIAN VILLAGE

Burns, Iroquois and Seminole Streets

Indian Village is a historic, tree-lined neighborhood of majestic homes that once belonged to Detroit's wealthy elite. You won't find any cookie-cutter homes here among the elegant Tudor, Federal, Beaux-Arts, Prairie, Gothic Revival and Neoclassic residences. The architecture is diverse, as various designers were employed to ensure completed homes reflected the individuality of the original homeowners and their status. According to the Historic Indian Village Association, while many of the homes fall into a distinct architectural style, elements from other styles were incorporated into the design to give each home a unique and eclectic look.

The subdivision was platted in 1895. A few homes date back to then, but most were constructed between 1900 and 1926. The multi-story homes are large, and many have ballrooms, grand staircases, butler pantries, carriage houses and all the amenities upscale homes of the era would possess.

Distinguished architects of the day designed the homes, including Albert Kahn, George D. Mason, Louis Kamper, C. Howard Crane and William Stratton. These names appear throughout this book, as they were the architects of prominent commercial buildings in Detroit as well.

Indian Village was home to affluent residents such as Henry Leland, the founder of Lincoln and Cadillac; Edsel Ford, president of Ford Motor Company and Henry Ford's son; Fritz Goebel, vice president of Goebel Brewing Company; George M. Holley, founder of Holley Carburetor; and John Kay, founder of Wright, Kay and Company.

The Historic Indian Village Detroit Home and Garden Tour is held in June of each year.

4. JOSEPH BERRY SUBDIVISION/MANOOGIAN MANSION

9240 Dwight Street

"Detroit like New York City provides an official residence for its Mayor," states a circa 1970s brochure distributed by the city's Department Report and Information Committee. "In New York City it is Gracie Mansion and in Detroit it is Manoogian Mansion."

The brochure describes the interior of the fifteen-room, three-thousand-square-foot Mediterranean-style mansion built in 1927 at an estimated cost of $65,000 as having seven bedrooms, nine baths, two patios, an outdoor swimming pool, a landscaped garden and grounds and a basement recreation room. The publication omits the basement bowling alley, boathouse and stunning array of arched, leaded and bowed windows, which provide an abundance of natural light and dramatic views of the Detroit River.

Other sources indicate the original owner of the mansion, located in the Joseph Berry historic district, lost the property during the Great Depression, which enabled industrialist Alex Manoogian, an Armenian immigrant and founder of Masco Corporation, to purchase it at auction in 1939 for a mere $25,000 after the house sat vacant for many years. Manoogian donated the residence to the city in 1965 to show appreciation to his adopted hometown where he enjoyed much success.

"Ping-pong diplomacy" took place at the mansion after President Richard Nixon's notable visit to the Peoples Republic of China in February 1972. Mayor Roman Gribbs and his wife, Katherine, hosted a dinner the following April for United Nations Chinese delegates and members of the Chinese ping-pong team.

In a two-page letter dated March 6, 1974, Mrs. Gribbs recounted that Detroit was the first U.S. stop on a three-week tour of the country, and the ping-pong players were the first visitors from China in over thirty years. Seventy-four guests in attendance were served a variety of ethnic foods and beverages, including the sparkling wine "Cold Duck, a Detroit invention, [and] Vernors Ginger Ale, also originating here." One of the local translators later told Mrs. Gribbs, "Of the 3 weeks the Chinese spent in North America, the evening at the Mansion was the most relaxing and enjoyable."

In 1974, Mayor Coleman A. Young entertained foreign leaders at the mansion in town for the World Economic Summit co-hosted by the mayor and President Gerald Ford.

5. WATERWORKS PARK

Jefferson Avenue and Cadillac Boulevard

The palatial-looking building in the background is a water pumping station. Can you believe it? In 1879, the City of Detroit built a grand park encompassing 110 acres of waterfront property that became one of the wonders of the world. This landmark was the subject of thousands of postcards and drew visitors from all over the world. Ironically, the site's purpose was utilitarian—to supply water to metropolitan Detroit—but water commissioners wanted the grounds to be used as a public park too.

The beautiful stand-pipe tower of the pumping station designed like a slender minaret was the stand-out attraction.

Hurlbut Memorial Gate served as the grand entrance to the opulent Waterworks Park, once a major tourist attraction. The gate and palace-like pumping station are the only remnants of the grandeur. *Author's collection.*

Inside the 185-foot-tall brick structure was an iron stairway circling the stand-pipe, which visitors could climb to capture grand views of the city from the balcony at the top of the 202 winding steps.

At one time, the park included a lagoon used for wading and navigating small sailboats, tennis courts, a floral clock, a baseball diamond, a picnic area and playground equipment. The park officially closed to the public in the 1960s. Vestiges of the park's former glory include the Beaux-Arts Hurlbut Memorial Gate and pumping station.

6. PEWABIC POTTERY

10125 East Jefferson Avenue

The Arts and Crafts movement began in England during the second half of the nineteenth century to counter what was perceived to be the mass production of cheap, lackluster and unoriginal examples of decorative arts. Pewabic Pottery is Detroit's contribution to what grew into an international movement that promoted craftsmanship and artistic vision over quantity and cost.

Michigan's only historic pottery began in 1902 after artist Mary Chase Perry experimented with firing and glazing ceramic works in a basement kiln belonging to her neighbor Horace James Caulkins, a dental supplier. Twenty-five years earlier, Caulkins had invented the Revelation kiln, a portable, high-temperature oven for firing dental enamel.

This encounter resulted in the two forming a partnership the following year and opening a studio located in a vacant carriage house behind the Ransom Gillis home in Brush Park. Their first customer, a Chicago business specializing in china and pottery, ordered $1,000 worth of bowls and lamps. Works produced were called either Miss Perry's Pottery or Revelation Pottery, according to the nonprofit's online timeline.

In 1904, the pottery was renamed Pewabic, an Ojibway word for metal and the name of a copper mine located in Perry's hometown of Hancock, Michigan, according to staff. Architectural tiles debuted in the product line, and commissions came in from around the country.

In need of a larger studio, Perry and Caulkins sought out design assistance from Stratton and Baldwin, a local architectural firm. Perry would eventually marry architect William Buck Stratton, a staunch supporter of the arts, and

Decorative Pewabic Pottery tiles, circa 1921, depict scenes from popular children's literature. The fireplace is one of many treasures inside the main library. *Rod Arroyo.*

become Mary Chase Perry Stratton. Pewabic Pottery would move into its new Tudor Revival studio in 1907, now a national historic landmark.

In 1909, a remarkable breakthrough occurred when Perry created an iridescent glaze that became the pottery's hallmark. This discovery established Pewabic as one of the most innovative potteries of its time.

Pewabic installations can be found in numerous homes, churches and commercial buildings throughout the United States, including the National Shrine of Immaculate Conception, Shedd Aquarium and Nebraska State Capitol. A few public examples in Detroit include the Detroit Public Library, Guardian Building, Cathedral Church of St. Paul, Comerica Park and Detroit People Mover stations.

Pewabic Pottery, a nonprofit since 1979, is open to the public. Visitors can purchase a variety of decorative items, including popular Detroit souvenir tiles, and see artists at work continuing the Pewabic legacy over a century after the collaboration between founders Perry and Caulkins began. Or they can create their own piece of history by participating in the many classes offered.

CITY OVERVIEW • SITES OF INTEREST

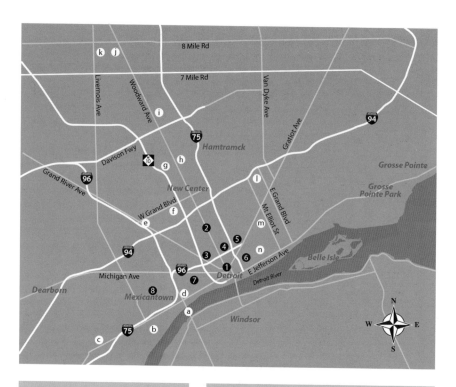

1. **Downtown**
2. **Midtown**
3. **Cass Park Historic District**
4. **Brush Park**
5. **Eastern Market**
6. **Lafayette Park**
7. **Corktown**
8. **Mexicantown**

a. Ambassador Bridge
b. Fort Wayne
c. Woodmere Cemetery
d. Ste. Anne de Detroit
e. Dabls MBAD African Bead Museum
f. Hitsville, USA / Motown Museum
g. Boston-Edison Historic District
h. Arden Park
i. Ford Highland Park Plant
j. Rosa Parks Crypt / Woodlawn Cemetery
k. Baker's Keyboard Lounge
l. Packard Plant
m. Heidelberg Project
n. Elmwood Cemetery

CHAPTER 6

CITY OVERVIEW

SITES OF INTEREST

1. DOWNTOWN (SEE CHAPTER 2)
2. MIDTOWN (SEE CHAPTER 3)

3. CASS PARK HISTORIC DISTRICT

MASONIC TEMPLE
500 Temple Street

The Roaring Twenties transformed Detroit's landscape as massive new skyscrapers sprouted up everywhere. While most building projects of the day garnered immense publicity, none could equal the fanfare extended during the construction of the world's largest Masonic temple.

Membership in Masonic fraternities surged at the onset of the twentieth century. To meet the needs of increased membership, the Masonic Temple Association of Detroit opted to go big and build new rather than enlarge its original temple on Lafayette Avenue. Architect George Mason designed an elaborate Gothic masterpiece constructed from Indiana limestone that consumed an entire city block in order to accommodate all the various bodies composing the organization. The ritualistic tower spanned fourteen stories, while the interior encompassed "some twelve million cubic feet of space in all, making it the largest and most complete building of all time."

In November 1920, an estimated twenty thousand master Masons and curious onlookers assembled across the street in Cass Park on Thanksgiving Day to witness the turning of the sod or groundbreaking ceremony. More pomp accompanied the laying of the cornerstone on September 18, 1922. The first mortar was spread with the same trowel used by our nation's first president, George Washington, in the laying of the cornerstone of the United States Capitol building in 1793. Washington became a Mason at age twenty, so the symbolism behind the use of his personal trowel and presence of his Mason's apron at this ceremony was huge.

The temple opened on November 26, 1926, to even more fanfare. Members of the Masonic order, twenty-five thousand strong, marched in a parade preceding the ceremony, while an estimated crowd of fifty thousand jammed Cass Park.

Temple plans included provisions for fifty Masonic bodies to operate independently, as well as two lavish auditoriums and ballrooms, a Commandery or Asylum that looks like it's straight out of King Arthur and the Knights of the Round Table, numerous lodges and many other rooms, several of which were never completed. One really needs to take a tour of the building to fully appreciate its enormity and grasp the meaning behind

The world's largest Masonic temple. George Washington's tools were used to lay the cornerstone. *Courtesy of Library of Congress.*

all the symbolism represented in the elaborate decorative elements found throughout the temple.

One major piece of symbolism appears in the conspicuous triptych above the main entrance defined by a triple doorway within a fine Gothic arch. The triptych displays three sculptural figures representing King Solomon, Hiram Abiff and Hiram (King of Tyre), builders of the "magnificent Temple to God that stands as the beginning of all Masonic activity."

4. BRUSH PARK

This historic neighborhood established in 1860 spans twenty-four blocks and was home to Detroit's upper crust during the later part of the nineteenth and early twentieth centuries. Residential development began in 1850 on the former French ribbon farm that stretched north from the Detroit River along Woodward Avenue after Edmund Brush inherited the estate from his father, Elijah Brush, a prominent local attorney and second mayor of incorporated Detroit.

Edmund divided the property and sold parcels to wealthy families who heeded strict building requirements by constructing large, expensive homes in a variety of architectural styles such as Victorian, Edwardian, Italianate and Gothic. French design influences were immensely popular then and coincided with grand efforts by France's emperor Napoleon III to modernize the capital city of Paris by replacing medieval buildings and narrow streets with monumental neo-classic structures and wide boulevards. Brush Park's many Second Empire–style homes with their charming mansard roofs reflect this trend. Hence, the elegant neighborhood soon became known as "Little Paris of the Midwest."

As commercial development encroached upon this once idyllic neighborhood and interest in architecture popular during the Gilded Age waned, residents bolted for newer, larger, more exclusive digs in Boston-Edison and Indian Village. Concurrently, Detroit's burgeoning auto industry created a demand for lower-income housing for the influx of workers migrating to the city. The stately mansions were converted into apartments, rooming houses and commercial spaces or bulldozed to make way for larger apartments or parking lots. This was the start of the decline of this once prosperous area, which became known as a skid row during the latter part of the twentieth century.

This area is under redevelopment and will look totally different in the next few years. The mansion built for dry goods merchant Ransom Gillis was renovated by Nicole Curtis, host of the popular HGTV and DIY television show *Rehab Addict*.

5. EASTERN MARKET

This popular marketplace is the largest historic market district in the United States, dating back to 1891. As the city grew, three major markets relocated to the German quarter on the outskirts of town, replacing the Russell Street Cemetery. The Silas Farmer & Co. *Illustrated Guide and Souvenir of Detroit* published thirteen years before the market's construction described, "The immense Lion Brewery near Russell Street, is a most noticeable landmark," as well as the "elegant" St. John's Lutheran Church and school, Trinity Lutheran Church and "the immense German Catholic St. Joseph's Cathedral, the largest church edifice in Detroit." The three churches referenced still stand, although St. John's is now St. John–St. Luke Evangelical Church and St. Joseph's is not a cathedral.

Another site to once behold, per the guide, was the Detroit House of Corrections, described as extensive and outwardly attractive. "Much time may profitably be spent here in tour of the buildings, shops and grounds. It is one of the largest and best managed institutions of its kind in the world, and has an average of 700 inmates, chiefly employed making chairs."

The market remains a bustling area today with wholesalers still servicing restaurants and grocery stores as they've done for more than a century. Thousands flock to the outdoor Saturday market, where farmers from Michigan and nearby states sell a variety of fresh produce, meats, cheeses and other delicacies. Flower Day, a time-honored spring tradition since 1967, takes place on the Sunday following Mother's Day and draws over 150,000 gardeners. In the summer, the outdoor public market runs on Tuesday and Thursday evenings as well.

The fourteen-acre market district has undergone many changes in recent years. Vacant warehouses and breweries have been converted into residential lofts and commercial spaces housing restaurants, galleries and retail stores. In the evenings, the produce sheds become beautiful event spaces where weddings and other private galas are hosted. Artists have plied their trades on the exterior of many buildings, creating a popular extensive

Consumers seeking out the freshest produce in one of the sheds at Eastern Market. *Rod Arroyo.*

outdoor art gallery that draws visitors as well. Since 2015, artists have created more than 125 murals as part of Murals in the Market, a collaborative art/community platform and mural festival. In 2018, the Smithsonian named Murals in the Market one of the best mural festivals in the world.

While change has been inevitable, concerted efforts are underway to preserve the historic purpose of the market too. For those who like to experience the market's history firsthand, dining at Roma Café, now Amore Detroit, the city's oldest Italian restaurant, is a great traditional option, as is munching on Germack pistachios. Germack Pistachio Company claims to be the oldest roaster of pistachios in the country. Enjoying Bloody Marys from Vivio's on Market Street is a longtime ritual, as are the jazz performances at Bert's Marketplace. Bert's even offers live music and karaoke on Saturday market days. Follow the beckoning smell of barbecue ribs and chicken grilling outdoors over charcoal to the Russell Street restaurant. Gratiot Central Market is a longtime carnivore favorite. Every part of the animal, from snout to rump, can be found at this popular inside hub of meat vendors.

6. LAFAYETTE PARK

Admirers of architect Mies Van der Rohe travel from all over the world to see this much-heralded urban renewal project of the 1950s, the largest collection of his work in one spot. The planned community features high-rise towers designed in the International style and low-slung two-story town homes surrounded by parks and greenery.

Lafayette Park's construction displaced thousands of the city's black residents from the neighborhood known as Black Bottom, named by the French for its rich soil. The subsequent construction of nearby I-375 destroyed their thriving commercial district known as Paradise Valley. Hastings Street, once longer than Bourbon Street and the heart of Paradise Valley, was populated by jazz and blues clubs that saw legends such as Johnny Lee Hooker performing there.

7. CORKTOWN (SEE CHAPTER 4)

8. MEXICANTOWN

While Detroit's population has declined over the last six decades, one southwest Detroit neighborhood overcame the decimating effects of population loss thanks to a new wave of immigrants from Mexico arriving in the city beginning in the 1940s and 1950s. Mexican immigrants settled

A street scene of the popular Bagley Avenue restaurant district in Mexicantown. *Rod Arroyo.*

in Detroit for the same reason previous ethnicities came here: to provide a better life for their families.

The influx of immigrants over the ensuing years resulted in a neighborhood that not only survived but thrived. By retaining aspects of their culture and customs, the area has also become a popular destination for non-Hispanic residents who delight in the colorful murals embellishing the exteriors of many businesses and authentic foods available from a variety of bakeries, markets, food trucks and restaurants.

Christened "Mexicantown" during a 1980s public relations campaign, this neighborhood spans many blocks, with Bagley Avenue and Vernor Highway home to many authentic Mexican-style dining hotspots. There are many gems off the beaten track too, so it may be wise to inquire among locals as to their favorite places.

A. AMBASSADOR BRIDGE

Ambassador Bridge Street (use exit 47B from either northbound or southbound I-75)

When the Ambassador Bridge opened in November 1929, it was a big deal. With a center span measuring 1,850 feet, this international bridge connecting the United States and Canada through border cities Detroit and Windsor was the largest suspension bridge in the world.

Everything about the bridge was big, including signage. Prior to its opening, a daily newspaper's headline proclaimed: "Signs of Blazing Letters 6 Feet High Serve as Guide to Bridge." Two main towers sporting the bridge name "emblazoned on the sky in fiery letters…nearly 400 hundred feet above the river" made it easy for motorists to find the bridge approaching it from either city. "So intense will the brilliancy of the Ambassador sign [be] that in clear weather the red glow will be plainly visible to the passengers on boats way out on Lake Erie and on boats when or soon after they pass the light where the St. Clair empties into Lake St. Clair."

Both the United States Congress and Canada's Parliament approved construction of the privately financed bridge, but Detroit mayor John W. Smith opposed it. Mayor Smith didn't think the international link should be privately owned with owners reaping all the profits. Controversy ensued between opposing parties. In June 1927, a special election was held. Detroit voters decided unanimously in favor of the private enterprise.

The George Washington Bridge, which spans the Hudson River between New York and New Jersey, claimed the title of longest suspension bridge in the world two years after the Ambassador opened. While the Ambassador Bridge ranks seventy-ninth today in terms of size, its importance remains. It's the number-one border crossing in North America in traffic and trade, per the Michigan Department of Transportation. The crossing is so busy that a second bridge has been deemed necessary to keep up with demand.

A peaceful riverfront scene of Detroit Renaissance Center, with Ambassador Bridge in background. *Rod Arroyo.*

Controversy surrounds construction of the second bridge as well. Representatives of the current owner of the bridge have filed numerous lawsuits to halt construction of the publicly owned bridge project because it will siphon profits from the private venture. Named after the legendary Canadian-born Detroit Red Wings hockey player, the Gordie Howe International Bridge's anticipated opening is 2022.

B. HISTORIC FORT WAYNE
6325 West Jefferson Avenue

Don't expect manicured lawns, slick interactive kiosks and interpretative centers like those found at other historic forts run by the National Park Service or other nonprofit organizations with substantial operational budgets when you visit. Maintained by the City of Detroit and volunteer partner organizations, Fort Wayne is rough in comparison. There is a certain charm, however, to be found walking among the fort's intact star configuration, ruins and semi-restored structures in this state as opposed to the overly polished historic sites that are more akin to amusement parks.

Named for General "Mad" Anthony Wayne, a Revolutionary War hero who may not be viewed so favorably by many today, the fort is located on the narrowest point of the Detroit River. It's one of several fortifications built by the United States government along the northern border in the 1840s as protection from possible British invasion. Detroit's proximity to Canada made it especially vulnerable.

The threat of British invasion waned by 1849, so the rustic earth and wood fort didn't see much action again until the American Civil War, when Fort Wayne was filled beyond capacity as volunteers mustered and trained for war. At this time, the earthen fortifications were rebuilt in masonry.

The fort never mounted its cannons, and to this day, no shots against enemies have been fired. Fort Wayne has served the military as a training center, home to infantry regiments, supply depot, prisoner of war camp and major induction center through the end of the Vietnam War. The fort served as a shipping point for thousands of tons of transportation-related supplies during World War II. The unemployed found work here building or rebuilding structures during the Great Depression, and those displaced in 1967 by civil unrest found a home.

It's hard to imagine a Fort Wayne so active and large that it required a hospital, post office, theater, jail and more. An ideal guide to navigating this

Detroit treasure is the Arcadia book *Detroit's Historic Fort Wayne*, listed in the bibliography found at the back of this book. If possible, purchase the book prior to your visit. The concise descriptions and accompanying photographs help shed light on Fort Wayne's role in Detroit and American history. The images put the remaining buildings in context within the different eras.

The fort hosts various events throughout the warmer months and is open to visitors on weekends. For more information, visit www.fortwaynecoalition.com.

c. Woodmere Cemetery
9400 West Fort Street

A stroll or drive through this historic cemetery established in 1867 in what was then a rural area on the outskirts of Detroit becomes another discovery of who's who in Detroit and Michigan history. Foremost cemetery designer Adolph Strauch, whose Spring Grove Cemetery in Cincinnati set the standard for cemetery construction at the time, created the plan for Woodmere.

A few examples of prominent politicians, industrialists, retailers and clergy buried here include John Bagley, Moses Field, James Vernor, Hamilton Carhartt, Seymour Finney, Dexter M. Ferry, David Whitney and Henry M. Leland.

Architect Albert Kahn's brother Moritz, considered an innovator in commercial building construction and credited with developing steel-reinforced concrete, is buried here, along with David Buick. Buick invented the bathtub enameling process and founded Buick Motor Car Company.

Private Eddie Slovik, the only World War II soldier executed for desertion, is buried here, as are four men killed in 1932 during a protest against Ford Motor Company in what's known as Ford Hunger March and Battle of the Overpass.

The cremains from the now-defunct Detroit Crematorium and Columbarium can be found inside the Donaldson and Meier–designed Gothic chapel and crematorium. In the late nineteenth and early twentieth centuries, cremation was not widely accepted. The Detroit Cremation Association advocated for its acceptance and built a crematorium near Woodmere Cemetery. By 1929, cremation had become an established burial tradition. The association closed and donated its cremains to Woodmere Cemetery. Incidentally, Woodmere began offering cremation services in 1913 and discontinued operations in 1999.

D. SAINTE ANNE DE DETROIT

1000 Sainte Anne Street

Worship at or visit a church whose history dates to Detroit's founding. On July 26, 1701, two days after Antoine de La Mothe Cadillac and his entourage stepped ashore in what would become Detroit, they erected the very first church. Construction coincided with the Feast of Saint Anne, which honors the mother of Mary; hence the name. From that day in July, Sainte Anne de Detroit (French spelling) has played a pivotal role in the city's history. Sainte Anne claims to be the second-oldest continuously operating Catholic parish in the United States. Cathedral Basilica of St. Augustine in Florida, where the first service took place on August 28, 1565, contends it's the first.

A historic marker in the Financial District located on the façade of 1 Griswold Street, a 1930s skyscraper built for Standard Savings and Loan, denotes the site of Sainte Anne's first church. When fire swept through the early settlement in 1703, the church, rectory and several other buildings were destroyed. Throughout Detroit's early history, Sainte Anne's parish moved several times until it settled in the eighth and current structure, built in 1886.

Several articles from the earlier churches are housed here, including the

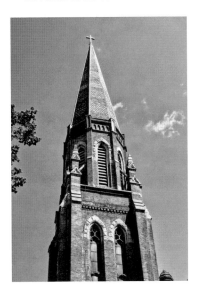

The parish of Sainte Anne de Detroit Catholic Church traces its roots back to the landing of Antoine de la Mothe Cadillac in July 1701. *Rod Arroyo.*

gray stained-glass windows at the top sides of the main sanctuary. These windows are the oldest in the city of Detroit, per Danielle Center, church historian and program director.

Most of the inscriptions in the windows are in French, a nod to the French settlers who worshiped here for generations. A single window in the back of the church inscribed in Spanish acknowledges the demographic of today's parishioner. According to Center, church attendance rapidly declined throughout the twentieth century, resulting in plans to shutter the historic church. In the 1960s, as talks of closing progressed, the neighborhood underwent a revival as another wave of Hispanic immigrants settled here. This influx of largely Catholic immigrants played a crucial role in keeping Sainte

Anne's open and enabling it to continue its religious tradition into the twenty-first century.

Sainte Anne's is the final resting place of Father Gabriel Richard, the parish's most famous pastor and one of Detroit's most influential early residents. His tomb lies in the small chapel behind the main altar. Born and ordained in France, he fled his homeland in the spring of 1792 following the rise of anti-clericalism during the French Revolution and sought refuge in the Sulpician community in Baltimore, Maryland. Within six months, Father Richard had been sent to an Illinois mission, where he worked alongside recent settlers and native people of the territory.

In 1798, he was reassigned to Detroit and became pastor of Sainte Anne de Detroit in 1802. Often referred to as Detroit's second founding father, the priest left an indelible mark on what would become his home for over three decades as cleric, teacher, innovator and politician. After a great fire destroyed the early settlement in 1805, he coined the phrase that would become the city motto: *Speramus meliora; resurgent cineribus*, or "We hope for better things; it shall arise from the ashes."

Father Richard is credited with bringing the first printing press to Detroit and publishing Michigan's first newspaper, the *Michigan Essay* or *Impartial Observer*. On August 26, 1817, he established the Catholepistemiad of Michigania along with Reverend John Monteith, a Presbyterian minister; William Woodbridge, secretary of the Michigan Territory; and Augustus B. Woodward, chief justice of the Michigan Territory. Richard and Monteith would be the first professors of this pioneering primary, secondary and higher education institution in the Michigan Territory that later was renamed University of Michigan. A historic marker affixed to the One Detroit parking structure located near the downtown intersection of East Congress and Bates Streets denotes the school's original location, which was razed in 1850 after the university's 1837 relocation to Ann Arbor. Father Richard also established schools for girls and indigenous children.

The first Catholic priest elected to United States Congress, Father Richard served one term from 1823 to 1825 in the House of Representatives as a non-voting delegate of the Michigan Territory. In this capacity, he gained federal support to build the territory's first road, now known as Michigan Avenue, which linked Detroit and Chicago, opening Michigan to settlement.

In 1832, a cholera epidemic swept through Detroit. While tending to the sick and dying, Father Richard contracted cholera and succumbed to this horrific disease on September 13, 1832, almost one month shy of his sixty-fifth birthday.

E. DABLS MBAD AFRICAN BEAD MUSEUM
6559 Grand River Avenue

Nearly two decades ago, Olayami Dabls settled on this location to begin a quiet revolution using handcrafted African beads and art to enlighten the community about the power of their African heritage. A visual storyteller for over forty-five years, Dabls conveys the stories about the human condition through works composed of iron, rock, wood and mirrors, materials he believes are primary building blocks that speak universally to all cultures.

A former artist-in-residence and curator at the Charles H. Wright Museum of African American History, Dabls discovered how challenging it was to talk about emotionally charged history such as the civil rights movement in this capacity. His experience led to the creation of this communal space where he could use sculpture and African artifacts to foster understanding of the African experience.

People come from all over the world to photograph themselves among the reflective glass mosaics covering several buildings, as well as eighteen outdoor art installations occupying a full city block. Thousands of handcrafted beads from Africa are available for sale inside the museum, each with its own story. If you're lucky, Dabls will be on hand to explain their significance as they relate to the past and present.

F. HITSVILLE, U.S.A./MOTOWN MUSEUM
2648 West Grand Boulevard

The Empire on West Grand Boulevard is hallowed ground when it comes to Detroit history and one of the most beloved local tourist attractions. People travel from around the globe to see where legends such the Supremes, Four Tops, Temptations, Marvin Gaye, Smokey Robinson and the Miracles, Stevie Wonder, Martha Reeves and the Vandellas, Glady Knight and the Pips, Lionel Ritchie, Commodores and Jackson 5 got their start. They're amazed to discover the gigantic Motown sound, heard and loved worldwide, began in this tiny bungalow.

The family of Berry Gordy, founder of Motown Records, migrated to Detroit from the South in the 1920s to escape racial strife and take advantage of the opportunities available in the auto industry. Gordy, born in 1929, even worked a stint on the assembly line. Reputedly, this experience inspired him to increase company profits by having different artists record the same song

The tiny first-floor studio inside this home is where the Motown sound was born and the empire on West Grand Boulevard began. Visitors from around the world convene on this local gem to relive the glory days of Motown. *Rod Arroyo*.

under his various record labels. The name Motown itself was derived from Motor City.

Gordy launched his record label and recording studio thanks to a loan from the family bank. The household practiced a form of venture capitalism whereby all members were required to get jobs at the age of fifteen and make regular contributions to the bank. Even spouses were required to contribute. Gordy pitched his idea before the family, requesting $1,000. He received $800. With the funds, Gordy started Tamla Records in 1958, forerunner to Motown Records. He then purchased this house on West Grand Boulevard; he and his wife lived in the upper flat and built a recording studio and office on the first floor. Gordy opened the studio in a house because he had no other options. Restrictive real estate covenants prevented most blacks from purchasing commercial buildings. They circumvented these discriminatory codes by starting businesses in homes. From this humble abode, Gordy churned out hit after hit and turned local teenagers into superstars.

The music scene prior to and through the 1950s and '60s was segregated. Motown broke down racial barriers and defined the term "crossover" when its stars appeared on popular television shows of the day such as *American Bandstand* and *The Ed Sullivan Show* and its songs were played on radio stations that catered to white audiences. The upbeat music had everybody singing along, regardless of race. Young girls imitated the Supremes. Boys wanted to be cool like Marvin Gaye, the Four Tops or the Temptations.

Thanks to the songwriting skill of Lamont Dozier and brothers Brian and Eddie Holland, who wrote, arranged and produced many of the songs from 1962 to 1967 that came to define the Motown sound, there was never a shortage of hits. In 1968, five Motown hits were in the top ten on *Billboard's*

Hot 100 chart. The label accomplished another unprecedented feat when it seized the top three spots for an entire month.

According to Motown history, it was the first African American record label to reach widespread national acclaim. The label broke down racial barriers by becoming the most successful independent record company in history and the most successful African American–owned business in America.

With over 180 number-one hits, Motown is an inspirational success story. One of the most enduring legacies of Motown, besides the hits, is that it brought about social change. Smokey Robinson once commented that when Motown began, its artists performed before segregated audiences in the South. Once Motown took off, they performed before integrated audiences with white kids and black kids standing next to one another dancing, clapping and singing along. It wasn't war or legislation that knocked down racial barriers—it was music that brought about this huge change. That music was made right here!

Gordy ended up purchasing seven neighboring homes and used them to house artist development, accounting and other administrative offices. While the buildings look much like they did when Motown first opened, change is underway. Plans to enlarge the museum and elevate it to the stature it deserves have begun. Luckily, renderings released thus far show the original Motown headquarters, home of Studio A, as a recognizable, stand-out feature of the new design.

G. Boston-Edison Historic District
Between Woodward Avenue and Linwood Street, Boston Boulevard and Edison Avenue

This historic neighborhood, a desirable location for wealthy and upwardly mobile homeowners in the early twentieth century, spans thirty-six blocks and contains nine hundred homes ranging from modest, two-story structures to impressive mansions, with most built between 1905 and 1925.

No two homes are alike, according to the Historic Boston-Edison Association, which claims to be the oldest continuously active neighborhood association in Detroit. While building restrictions dictated some uniformity as to scale, rooflines, setbacks and either stone or brick exteriors, architectural diversity was encouraged. Here you'll find fine examples of homes built in English, Roman, Greek or Colonial Revival, French Provincial, Italian Renaissance and Prairie styles, as well as unique interpretations of them.

The quiet, sedate neighborhood featuring streets lined with arching American elms and landscaped boulevards beckoned industrialists, artists, merchants, politicians, religious leaders and sports heroes seeking refuge from the noisy, crowded and dirty ever-expanding city core.

Early residents included automotive pioneer Henry Ford and his wife, Clara; Detroit Symphony Orchestra conductor Ossip Gabrilowitsch and his wife, Clara Clemens, daughter of author Samuel Clemens (Mark Twain); retailer Sebastian S. Kresge, founder of S.S. Kresge Company, a popular national dime or variety store chain originating in Detroit; union labor leader Walter P. Reuther; actor Brace Beemer, radio voice of *The Lone Ranger*; and baseball and boxing legends Ty Cobb and Joe Louis. Visitors frequently request a "drive by" of the Boston Avenue mansion built for real estate developer Nels Michelson and later purchased by Motown founder Berry Gordy.

While the list of prominent residents is too long to include here in its entirety, self-guided walking or driving tour itineraries featuring addresses of luminaries who once lived in the neighborhood can be downloaded at www.historicbostonedison.org.

H. ARDEN PARK—EAST BOSTON HISTORIC DISTRICT
East Boston Boulevard and Arden Park Boulevard
between Woodward and Oakland Avenues

Like adjacent Boston-Edison, this prestigious, planned neighborhood with ninety-two custom-built homes appealed to affluent homeowners. Touted as the "Highest Class Residence Property in the City" by the North Avenue Land Company in a May 25, 1913 *Detroit Free Press* advertisement, the neighborhood featured a beautiful parkway extending the length of the subdivision, with hundreds of fine shade trees of different varieties planted throughout and resident-owned, private parks located at the Woodward Avenue entrance. All building plans needed to be preapproved, with only single-family homes allowed. Properties were marketed toward purchasers who planned to reside here, not speculators. Residents had a say in selecting neighbors, as they were informed of prospective purchases before deals closed.

Early residents included automobile pioneers Frederic Fisher and John Dodge and merchants Clayton and Albert Grinnell, J.L. Hudson and Stanley Kresge Jr. Neither Arden Park nor Boston-Edison utilized restrictive real estate covenants, which were prevalent at the time, to exclude potential residents based on religion or race.

An impressive Arden Park landmark is the Cathedral of the Most Blessed Sacrament, the seat of the archbishop of Detroit, at 9844 Woodward Avenue. The exterior of the Norman Gothic–style cathedral designed by architect Henry A. Walsh of Cleveland, Ohio, was completed in 1915 and the interior in 1930. In 1938, Detroit was elevated to an archdiocese, and Most Blessed Sacrament Parish became the Cathedral of the Most Blessed Sacrament by decree of Pope Pius XI.

1. Ford Highland Park Plant
15050 Woodward Avenue, Highland Park

The red brick building is vacant and the sprawling factory behind it is in ruin—a sad fate for what many automotive historians consider one of the most significant industrial buildings in America.

According to the National Park Service:

> *Probably no factory changed life in 20th century America as much as the Highland Park Ford Plant. It was here, that Henry Ford and his engineers developed many of the crucial principles of modern mass production. The most notable of these was the continuously moving assembly line; its introduction in late 1913 reduced the assembly time of a Model T from 728 to 93 minutes. By 1920 the plant turned out a car every minute, and one out of every two automobiles in the world was a Model T.*

The innovation enabled Ford to implement the five-dollar workday, resulting in much higher wages and enabling workers to buy the cars they built.

Designated a National Historic Landmark in 1978, the factory's design was revolutionary too. Detroit architect Albert Kahn, who would become the nation's leading industrial architect, incorporated open floor plans and large windows in the design of this factory composed of a series of brick, concrete and steel buildings. The open floor plan allowed for efficient machinery placement with the potential for expansion. The large windows took advantage of the natural light to create a more pleasant and productive work environment. These features would become the standard for factory design.

Shift change at Ford Motor Company's Highland Park Plant. It was here that the moving assembly line and the five-dollar-per-day wage were introduced. *Courtesy of Library of Congress.*

The automated assembly line introduced in 1913 at the Highland Park Ford Plant revolutionized manufacturing. *Courtesy of Library of Congress.*

While the Highland Park Plant, which comprised offices, factories, a power plant and a foundry, was cutting-edge when first built, Ford needed a larger facility. Before auto production shifted to the new River Rouge Plant in Dearborn, an estimated fifteen million Model Ts rolled off the assembly line in Highland Park.

The Woodward Avenue Action Association purchased the building in 2014 with hopes of opening up an automotive welcome center. Unable to acquire financing, the organization scrapped the plan in 2016 and is seeking other development possibilities.

J. ROSA PARKS CRYPT/WOODLAWN CEMETERY
19775 Woodward Avenue

The mother of the modern civil rights movement is interred inside the Rosa L. Parks Freedom Chapel, located near the entrance of Woodlawn Cemetery, alongside her husband, Raymond, and mother, Leona McCauley. Parks's arrest after failing to relinquish her seat to a white passenger on a Montgomery, Alabama bus in December 1955 and her subsequent refusal to pay the fine spurred a citywide, 382-day transit boycott that led to the repeal of laws sanctioning segregation on public buses. Subjected to harassment and the inability to secure employment following this landmark decision, Parks, her husband and her mother moved to Detroit, where she resided until her death at age ninety-two in 2005. In 1996, President Bill Clinton presented Parks with the Presidential Medal of Freedom, the nation's highest civilian award, and during the 106th Congress (1999–2001), she received the Congressional Gold Medal. After her death, Parks became the first woman, second black American and third private citizen to lie in honor in the Rotunda of the United States Capitol.

Established in 1895, this 140-acre cemetery is rich in history. The Egyptian-style mausoleum belonging to Horace and John Dodge, the brothers behind their automotive namesake, is a must-see. Prominent burials include Edsel Ford, former Ford Motor Company president and son of Henry Ford; Reverend Clarence "C.L." Franklin, father of singer Aretha Franklin; and Hazen Pingree, beloved mayor of Detroit and Michigan governor. The graves of Motown legends Levi Stubbs and David Ruffin, lead singers of the Four Tops and Temptations, are here, as is a commemorative cenotaph dedicated to the King of Pop Michael Jackson. Most recently, the Queen of Soul Aretha Franklin was buried here.

Woodlawn Cemetery is known for its assemblage of "private estates" or elaborate mausoleums, which, even in death, exalt the worldly prosperity and stature of those interred inside.

Opposite the cemetery, east of Woodward Avenue, is where the Michigan State Fair used to be held. The annual fair ran from late August through Labor Day weekend beginning in 1905 until 2009. It was the end-of-summer highlight for many. Only a few buildings from the fair era still stand.

Power couple and noted philanthropists Thomas Witherell Palmer and his wife, Lizzie Pitts Merrill Palmer, donated a portion of their estate to the state specifically for use as fairgrounds. The grandson of Michigan's third territorial judge, James Witherell, Palmer served as United States senator from 1883 to 1889 and as minister to Spain after his 1889 appointment by President Benjamin Harrison. The president of the 1893 World's Columbian Exposition in Chicago, Palmer was the first president of both the Michigan Society for the Prevention of Cruelty to Animals (now Michigan Humane Society) and the Detroit Museum of Arts (now Detroit Institute of Arts). The Palmers are regarded by many as one of the most influential Detroit couples of the late nineteenth and early twentieth centuries.

South of the cemetery is Palmer Woods, a prestigious historic neighborhood developed on property once part of the Palmer estate. After Thomas Palmer died in 1913, Clarence Burton purchased the property for residential development. Noted landscape architect Ossian Simonds laid out the tree-lined curving streets in this circa 1915 subdivision where major executives from growing industries resided in opulence. Palmer Woods received the Michigan Horticulture Award of Merit in 1938 for being the finest platted subdivision in the state.

Noteworthy homes include the sixty-two-room Bishop Gallagher residence, built in 1925 by the Fisher brothers and gifted to the Archdiocese of Detroit bishop Michael Gallagher; and the Turkell-Bendow house, designed by Frank Lloyd Wright. Former Massachusetts governor and 2012 Republican presidential candidate Mitt Romney grew up in this neighborhood. His father, George W. Romney, was chairman of the now defunct American Motors Corporation and Michigan's forty-third governor. The house no longer stands.

Nearby Palmer Park was created on 140 acres donated to the city by the Palmers for use as a public park. During special events, visitors can enter the Palmers' fancy Mason and Rice–designed, two-story, 1885 log cabin appointed with an ornate carved grand staircase, two large fireplaces, beautiful stained-glass windows and modern amenities such as an indoor toilet and Jewel stove. The once stately and spectacular white marble Merrill fountain—commissioned by Lizzie Palmer in 1901 to honor her father, Charles Merrill—stands ravaged by time, vandals and neglect. Designed by well-known New York architects John Carrere and Thomas Hastings, the fountain stood in front of the Detroit Opera House at Campus Martius. It was moved to Palmer Park in 1925, when Woodward Avenue was widened, and has sat dry for over half a century. Hopefully a twenty-first-century philanthropist will step forth as the Palmers did and help the Friends of Palmer Park with its restoration.

FUN FACTS

1. Salt mines run beneath most of southwest Detroit.
2. Detroit claims the oldest continuously operating hat store (Henry the Hatter) and bowling alley (the Garden Bowl).
3. While the average American consumes four pounds of potato chips annually, Detroiters consume seven pounds.
4. The heat billowing from tubes and sidewalks around the city are called thermal leaks. A heating network called "district steam" exists underground in certain parts of the city and serves over one hundred buildings. The system, which dates to 1903 and consists of over fifty miles of steam mains, is notable for its age and size. When the steam pipes and cold external air come in contact, heat quickly escapes, causing these thermal leaks.

K. BAKER'S KEYBOARD LOUNGE
20510 Livernois Avenue

Experience history rather than read about it! Stop by Baker's Keyboard Lounge for a night out and enjoy great music in the oldest continuously operating jazz club in the world. Known for its superb acoustics and intimate setting,

Baker's has hosted a bevy of jazz and blues greats, including Cab Calloway, Ella Fitzgerald, George Shearing, Joe Williams, Maynard Ferguson, Miles Davis, Nat King Cole, Oscar Peterson, Sarah Vaughn, Woody Herman and many more. The legendary piano-shaped bar with its painted top mimicking a keyboard is a must-see and serves as a popular photo backdrop.

Baker's began as a sandwich shop in 1933, with spouses Chris and Fannie Baker serving the lunchtime crowd from a plain cement-block building located in what was then considered a rural part of the city. To boost off-hour business, the couple decided to add entertainment and enlisted their son Clarence to help line up jazz pianists for evening shows.

Food was the mainstay of the operation until 1939, when Clarence assumed ownership after his father suffered a stroke. Clarence chose to cultivate the music side by bringing in out-of-town pianists and regularly featuring Detroit-born jazz pianist Pat Flowers. His strategy worked, and the restaurant became known for its cutting-edge entertainment.

This newfound popularity resulted in an expansion and renovation in 1952 and a change in name to Baker's Keyboard Lounge. The larger floor plan increased the club's seating capacity, giving Clarence the leverage needed to book national acts such as Art Tatum, Dave Brubeck and Gerry Mulligan. At this time, modern elements were incorporated into the interior design, creating the sexy lounge vibe still intact today. Noteworthy features included the distinctive keyboard motif bar, tilted mirrors that allowed patrons to see the hands of pianists as they performed on the new Steinway piano (a gift from none other than one of the greatest jazz pianists of all time, Art Tatum) and the Art Deco–style paintings by Harry Julian Carew of major European cities that grace the walls.

You might also want to check out the club's original pricelist from 1934, when patrons could enjoy a beer for only twenty-six cents. Whether seated in the curved banquettes lining the club's perimeter, at the small tables next to the bandstand—where almost every jazz musician of national stature has played—or at the bar, there's no bad seat in the house.

Designated a Michigan historic site in 1986 and granted historic district status by the city in 2016, this venerable landmark has weathered its share of ups and downs since its heyday. Because of its storied past, Baker's Keyboard Lounge continues to assert considerable cachet and remains a popular spot for those wishing to step back in time and those who want to witness jazz greats of a new generation.

Reservations are a must, as seating is limited. For further information, visit theofficialbakerskeyboardlounge.com.

L. PACKARD PLANT
East Grand Boulevard and Concord Avenue

In 1902, local financier and industrialist Henry Bourne Joy and a group of investors became majority stakeholders in the Ohio Automobile Company, which they renamed Packard Motor Car Company. As company president, Joy moved Packard to Detroit and into the sprawling 3.5-million-square-foot factory located on forty acres spanning both sides of East Grand Boulevard. Considered the most advanced automobile factory in the world at the time, the factory was designed by Albert Kahn and built using reinforced concrete, the first time this method was used in the United States in an industrial capacity.

In this modern facility, skilled craftsmen representing over eighty trades built luxury cars regarded for many years as the "pride of the American automobile industry." A 1931 advertisement geared "for a discriminating clientele" stated that during the previous year, "nearly twice as many Packards were sold in foreign lands as any other car costing over $2,000. Abroad as at home, Packard dominates the fine car market."

During World War II, consumer automobile production ceased, and engines for bombers and other military equipment were built at the plant. It was the retooling of automotive plants for military production that earned Detroit the name "Arsenal of Democracy." When the war ended, automobile production resumed. By then, Packard Motor Car faced stiff competition from Cadillac and couldn't reach previous sales levels. Looking to cut production costs, the manufacturer merged with Studebaker. Packard-

An early 1900s view from East Grand Boulevard of the state-of-the-art Packard Motors automobile factory. A Detroit Publishing Company photo. *Courtesy of Library of Congress.*

A graphic wrap installed in 2015 over the Packard Plant's pedestrian bridge spanning East Grand Boulevard provides a glimpse of what it looked like in the 1930s. *Author's collection.*

Studebaker became the fourth-largest auto manufacturer in the country, but the merger didn't bode well for financially struggling Studebaker. In 1956, Packard production in Detroit ceased. While Studebaker would continue making Packards in South Bend, Indiana, until 1958, many consider the final model produced in Detroit on June 25, 1956, to be the last true Packard.

Other manufacturing or storage enterprises continued operating inside the massive complex after automobile production ended. A chemical processing company remained until 2010. Those businesses weren't enough to keep the place in working order, and the plant rapidly deteriorated. The once celebrated factory became a playground for graffiti artists, metal scrappers and urban explorers. Spanish investor Fernando Palazuelo purchased the sprawling factory for less than $500,000 in 2013. Security officers now patrol the property to keep trespassers at bay, and some renovations are underway. In 2017, the Packard plant's owner, Arte Express Detroit, began offering tours through local retail store Pure Detroit.

M. HEIDELBERG PROJECT
Heidelberg and Mount Elliot Streets

Artist Tyree Guyton has garnered worldwide recognition for this unique outdoor urban art installation created on the block where he grew up and was inspired in the arts by his grandfather Sam Mackey. The Heidelberg Project began in 1986, when Guyton took a paintbrush to the family home, covering it with a funky polka-dot motif. After returning from military service, Guyton was dismayed to see how the neighborhood had deteriorated in his absence. It was as if a bomb erupted is how he described his homecoming in multiple media interviews. Using art as his weapon, Guyton waged a personal war against urban blight on Detroit's east side.

Using what he and others euphemistically call "found objects," Guyton created small vignettes with political messages in his yard and a nearby vacant lot. With the help of neighborhood children and volunteers, Guyton transformed the neighborhood into a living indoor/outdoor gallery that now takes up a full city block and more.

Art or junk? That's the proverbial question visitors contemplate when strolling through this popular attraction described by the nonprofit in the following way: "Elements of the canvas contain recycled materials and found objects, most of which were salvaged from the streets of Detroit. Each work of art is carefully devised to tell a story about current issues plaguing society."

Artsy types embrace the unleashed creativity and thoughtfully ponder the significance of each vignette. Others shake their heads in disbelief and see only junk strewn haphazardly.

Mayors Coleman A. Young and Dennis Archer weren't keen on the project and tried to raze it during their administrations. Despite demolition attempts and arsonists' efforts to destroy it, the Heidelberg Project endures. In 2016, after a thirty-year run, Guyton announced the installation had served its purpose and would be dismantled in forthcoming years. He hinted at something new rising in its place. Currently, the Heidelberg Project remains intact and open to visitors. When visiting, be mindful that you're in a neighborhood with people residing in the surrounding houses. Not all neighbors enjoy the onslaught of visitors, so heed the No Trespassing signs posted on their property.

N. ELMWOOD CEMETERY
1200 Elmwood Street

The list of those buried at this state-designated historic site reads like a who's who in Detroit and Michigan history. Statesmen, scientists, actors, abolitionists, soldiers, industrialists, inventors, musicians and ordinary citizens are buried here.

A few notables include Lewis Cass, second territorial governor of Michigan, United States senator, ambassador to France and secretary of war; Winifred Lee Brent Lyster, author of state song "Michigan, My Michigan"; Eber Brock War, Detroit's first millionaire; Coleman A. Young,

Detroit's first black mayor, elected an unprecedented five times to this position; and Fred "Sonic" Smith, guitarist for the rock group the MC5.

Dedicated on October 8, 1846, Elmwood Cemetery encompassed forty-two acres, once part of the George Hunt farm located in Hamtramck Township, then a suburb of Detroit. Over the years, more land was acquired. Currently, Elmwood spans approximately eighty-six acres.

In 1890, prominent landscape architect Frederick Law Olmsted was hired to improve the cemetery's appearance and flow. The design he used was modeled after Mount Auburn Cemetery in Massachusetts, and the majestic, mature trees and lush vegetation encountered today stem from this plan. These tree plantings played a major role in the historic cemetery becoming Detroit's first certified arboretum in 2015.

A creek running through the cemetery represents the city's early topography. Named Parent's Creek in 1702 after an early French settler, it was renamed Bloody Run Creek after the ambush of Captain James Dalzell, a British officer, and his contingent of 260 soldiers by Native Americans as they attempted a surprise attack on Chief Pontiac's encampment during the 1763 Siege of Detroit known as Pontiac's Uprising or Pontiac's War. A Michigan historic marker indicates that Dalzell and 60 of his men died and states, "This battle marked the height of Pontiac's siege of Detroit, a struggle which he was forced to abandon three months later."

The creek ran red after so many dead and dying fell into the water, and from that time on, it was called Bloody Run Creek, wrote Frank and Arthur Woodford in *All Our Yesterdays*. Inside the cemetery remains the only visible portion of the creek.

ETCETERA

OTHER SITES OF INTEREST OUTSIDE GREATER DOWNTOWN DETROIT AREA NOT INCLUDED ON MAPS

JOHN K. KING USED AND RARE BOOKS

901 West Lafayette

Voted one of the world's best bookstores, this multi-story former glove factory has over one million books and an unprecedented collection of rare and collectors editions.

THE PARADE COMPANY

9500 Mount Elliott Street, Studio A

Get a behind-the-scenes look inside the 200,000-square-foot studio where artisans create the magical floats for the award-winning annual America's Thanksgiving Parade, a local tradition enjoyed since 1924 and started by the J.L. Hudson Company.

SOLANUS CASEY CENTER/ST. BONAVENTURE MONASTERY

1780 Mount Elliott Street

People visit the center to partake in spiritual reflection and healing. It's named for Blessed Solonus Casey, the monastery's porter, who is believed to have possessed the special gift of healing. Casey died in 1957 and was beatified on November 18, 2017, in a Mass held at Ford Field with seventy thousand people in attendance. Beatification is the step before canonization in the Catholic process for becoming a saint, which requires the recognition that a miracle has occurred due to the intercession of the individual. Blessed Casey is only the second American-born male to reach this status.

SHRINE OF THE BLACK MADONNA OF THE PAN AFRICAN ORTHODOX CHURCH

7625 Linwood Street

Shock and controversy accompanied the 1967 unveiling of Glanton Dowdell's eighteen-foot painting depicting Jesus and Madonna as black, as it contradicted the Western Christian narrative, which portrays Christ as a white man. The iconic painting prominently displayed in the chancel, coupled with the sermons of then pastor Reverend Albert Cleage Jr., turned the church into a political and social force promoting black independence and political power. The church played a vital role in electing the city's first African American mayor.

REDFORD THEATRE/ARTIST VILLAGE DETROIT

17360 Lahser Road

The continuous operation of this neighborhood movie palace since it opened in 1928 helped stave off the deterioration and subsequent demolition that became the fate of so many theaters around the country. The original Barton pipe organ is intact, making it one of two metro Detroit theaters still in possession of their original organs. It is owned by the Motor City Theatre

Organ Society, and a regular schedule of classic movies, independent films and organ concerts keeps this theater going. Outside the theater, take in all the cool murals that are part of Artist Village Detroit, a program that uses the arts to revitalize the neighborhood.

ROUGE PARK

Joy Road

Detroit's largest park is a 1,181-acre greenspace featuring playgrounds, a golf course, swimming pools, sports fields and Buffalo Soldiers Heritage Center. Enjoy visiting the butterfly garden or walking a path through fifteen acres of restored native prairie. The park suffered during Detroit's financial downturn, but improvements have been made and are still underway.

POPULAR ATTRACTIONS LOCATED IN SUBURBAN METRO DETROIT AND SOUTHEAST MICHIGAN YOU WON'T WANT TO MISS

Cranbrook (Bloomfield Hills)
Arab American Museum (Dearborn)
Fairlane Estate (Dearborn)
The Henry Ford/Greenfield Village/Ford Rouge Plant Tour (Dearborn)
Holocaust Memorial Center (Farmington Hills)
Edsel and Eleanor Ford House (Grosse Pointe)
Westcroft Gardens (Grosse Ile)
Selfridge Military Air Museum (Harrison Township)
General George A. Custer Exhibit, Monroe County Historical Museum (Monroe)
War of 1812 Battlefield National Park (Monroe)
Meadow Brook Hall (Rochester Hills)
Detroit Zoo (Royal Oak)
Michigan Firehouse Museum (Ypsilanti)
Yankee Air Museum (Ypsilanti)
Ypsilanti Automotive Heritage Museum (Ypsilanti)

James Scott Memorial Fountain.
Belle Isle Park, Detroit, Mich. 14

An artistic rendition of the James Scott Memorial Fountain on a vintage postcard. The white marble fountain is still a showpiece and popular photo backdrop for weddings. *Author's collection*.

BIBLIOGRAPHY

Barnstead, Elizabeth Wong. "Built in 1867, Most Holy Trinity's Organ Stood the Test of Time." *Michigan Catholic*, November 26, 2014.

Beal, Graham W.J. "Mutual Admiration, Mutual Exploitation: Rivera, Ford and the Detroit Industry Murals." *Berkeley Review of Latin American Studies*, University of California, 2010.

Beck, Don. "Can't Deny Detroit Has Spirit." *Detroit Free Press*, September 21, 1958.

Bulanda, George. "The Way It Was." *Hour Detroit*, January 8, 2015.

City of Detroit City Council. "The Proposed Historic Detroit Financial District Final Report." Historic Designation Advisory Board, October 5, 2010.

Conway, James, and David Jamroz. *Detroit's Historic Fort Wayne*. Charleston, SC: Arcadia Publishing, 2007.

Detroit Free Press. "Signs of Blazing Letters 6 Feet High Serve as Guide to Bridge." February 24, 1929.

Detroit News. "Those Daring Newsmen in Their Flying Machines." October 18, 2000.

Gavrilovich, Peter, and Bill McGraw, eds. *The Detroit Almanac*. Detroit, MI: Detroit Free Press, 2006.

Ghausi, Marilyn. "The Building/Paul Phillipe Cret Records 1919–1931." August 1980, Dalnet.lib.mi.us.

Gonyea, Don. "Detroit Industry: The Murals of Diego Rivera." NPR Special Series: Remaking Michigan, Retooling Detroit, April 22, 2009.

Hershenzon, Gail D. Images of America: *Detroit's Woodmere Cemetery*. Charleston, SC: Arcadia Publishing, 2006.

Hill, Eric J., and John Gallager. *AIA Detroit: The American Institute of Architects Guide to Detroit Architecture*. Detroit, MI: Wayne State University Press, 2003.

Historic American Buildings Survey, Mid-Atlantic Region, National Park Service Department of Interior. "East Ferry Avenue Historic District." Compiled after 1933.

The Hudson-Webber Foundation. "7.2 SQ MI: A Report on Greater Downtown Detroit." February 2015.

Hughes, Daphne. "History of the Manoogian Mansion." *Michigan Chronicle*, November 2016.

Ingall, David, and Karin Risko. *Michigan Civil War Landmarks*. Charleston, SC: The History Press, 2015.

Loomis, Bill. "Irish Helped Form Detroit for Centuries." *Detroit News*, March 15, 2015.

———. *On This Day in Detroit History*. Charleston, SC: The History Press, 2016.

Marzejka, Laurie J. "Detroit's Waterworks Park a Gateway to the Past." *Detroit News*, June 13, 2000.

Mazzei, Rebecca. "Paint for the People." *Detroit Metro Times*, July 14. 2004.

Mitchell, Gail. "Smokey Robinson Celebrates 50 Years by 'Having Fun.'" *Lifestyle*, August 21, 2009.

Oberholtzer, Michele. "What's the Source of the Steam Pouring out of Detroit's Sidewalks?" *Hour Detroit*, February 12, 2018.

Risen, James. "It's Thumbs Down for 'Fist' in Detroit." *Los Angeles Times*, October 16, 1978.

Schwartz, Larry. "Brown Bomber Was Hero to All." ESPN.com special, n.d.

Smith, Terry. *Making the Modern: Industry, Art, and Design in America*. Chicago: University of Chicago Press, 1993.

Spratling, Cassandra. "King's 1963 Walk to Freedom Still Inspires Detroit." *Detroit Free Press*, June 19, 2013.

U.S. House of Representatives. "The Honoring of Civil Rights Icon Rosa Parks." *History, Art & Archives*, June 13, 2016.

Warikoo, Niraj. "Detroit's Black Madonna Turned Church into Social Political Force." *Detroit Free Press*, April 27, 2017.

Weber, Charles C. "City-County Building Statue 14 Feet Tall, Weighs 8 Tons." *Detroit Free Press*, April 3, 1955.

Woodford, Frank B., and Arthur M. Woodford. *All Our Yesterdays: A Brief History of Detroit*. Detroit, MI: Wayne State University Press, 1969.

Websites

CMGWW.com (official Joe Louis website)

DetroitHistorical.org (Encyclopedia of Detroit)

DetroitTransitHistory.org

HistoricDetroit.org

History.com (This Day in History—1956 Last Packard Produced)

HistoryPlace.com (Irish Potato Famine)

PalmerPark.org

PBS.org (American Experience)

INDEX

INDEX

INDEX

INDEX

INDEX

ABOUT THE AUTHOR AND PHOTOGRAPHER

Detroit native KARIN RISKO is the owner of City Tour Detroit, formerly Hometown History Tours. She enjoys learning about new developments underway in the city, as well as continually uncovering juicy historical tidbits. The former history teacher earned a bachelor's degree in secondary education with a major in history from Central Michigan University. Karin is the coauthor of another History Press publication, *Michigan Civil War Landmarks*. Learn more about Karin at CityTourDetroit.com.

RODNEY L. ARROYO is a photographer with City Photos and Books, Inc., and Portraits by Rod. Rod began his photography career as a photojournalist, working for a daily newspaper in Florida. In 2002, he started his photography business in Michigan and has published several books of city images featuring locations including Washington, D.C.; Birmingham, Michigan; and Royal Oak, Michigan. Rod is also a partner in Giffels Webster, a multidisciplinary, community-building consulting firm, and he has served as an adjunct faculty member at Wayne State University in Detroit. Learn more about Rod at CityPhotosAndBooks.com.

Visit us at
www.historypress.com